Eternal Wisdom
Volume 1

ETERNAL WISDOM
Upadeshamritam

VOLUME 1

Compiled by
SWAMI JNANAMRITANANDA PURI

*English translation from the orginal Malayalam
by*
Dr. M.N. Namboodiri

Amrita Enterprises Private limited
Amritapuri, Kerala, India

ETERNAL WISDOM - Volume 1
Collection of Amma's Teachings
by Swami Jnanamritananda Puri

Published by:
Amrita Books
Amrita Enterprises Private Limited
Vallikavu P.O., Kollam 690 525, Kerala, India

First Edition 2019:1000 copies
Second Edition 2022 : 1000 copies

Copyright © 2003 by Mata Amritanandamayi Mission Trust All rights reserved. No part of this publication may be stored in a retrieval system, transmitted, reproduced, transcribed or translated into any language, in any form, by any means without the prior agreement and written permission of the publisher.

For more information contact:
Email: info@amritabooks.in
Website: www.amritabooks.in

Ashram Website:
www.amritapuri.org
www.amritaworld.org
www.embracingtheworld.org

ISBN 978-93-88246-62-0
₹220

MOTHER...

Let my every action

Be a worship of You

With total self-surrender,

Let every sound falling from my lips

Be a chant of Your great mantra,

Let each movement of my hands

Be a mudra in worship of You,

Let every step I take

Be a circumambulation of You,

Let all my food and drink

Be offerings in Your sacred fire,

Let my repose

Be a prostration to You.

Mother, let each act of mine,

And every comfort,

Be a worship of You.

Contents

FOREWORD	10
CHAPTER ONE	17
Monday, June 3, 1985	17
The Mother who never rests	17
Advice to householders	19
Leading a spiritual life to purify one's conduct	21
Monday, June 10, 1985	23
The Guru's instructions	24
Abode of compassion	26
Bhakti yoga	30
The importance of the right attitude	33
For spiritual seekers	34
The danger of wealth	35
Mother of the Universe	39
Meditation	48
The sorrows of worldly life	49
Details of sadhana	50
Advice to householders	54
CHAPTER TWO	81
Devotion	81
The nature of the Guru	83
Sadhana is indispensable	84
The greatness of devotion	86
Mother's instructions	89
Manasa puja (mental worship)	92
Friday, July 5, 1985	93
The principles of spiritual life	95
Monday, July 8, 1985	101
The happiness and sorrow of worldly life	102
No compromise in the discipline	104
Mother's cow seva	107

Advice to householders	109
Tuesday, August 6, 1985	114
Mother's divine mood of bhakti	116
The past is a cancelled check	118
The cause of sorrow and the remedy	120

CHAPTER THREE — 123

Wednesday, August 7, 1985	123
Meditation	123
She who removes all dangers	124
Is the future predestined?	126
Saturday, August 10, 1985	129
The spiritual journey	130
Monday August 12, 1985	136
Saturday, August 24, 1985	138
Clearing the doubts of the brahmacharis	139
Experiences that evoke wonder	143
The tireless Mother	145
Explanation of mission work	147
Unniyappam	150
Friday, September 6, 1985	153
The renunciate and relatives	154
On the seashore	157
Instructions to the brahmacharis	158
Memories of Mother's childhood	164

CHAPTER FOUR — 167

Friday, 20 September 1985	167
Brahmacharis and householders	167
A few moments with the brahmacharis	172
Feeding Her children	174
Amma with Ottoor	177
Seva and sadhana	178
Non-duality in daily life	181
A cooking lesson	183

Mother blesses a cow	184
Worshipping the deities and the Guru	185
Sunday, October 13, 1985	188
Follow the principle behind rituals	190
How to face blame and praise	193
A mishap caused by a dog	195
The Mother who bestows unseen blessings	198
The treasure inside	200
Initiation from the Goddess of learning	202
Give to those who are in need	205
No poverty for the true devotee	207
Put your faith into action	209
Faith in God and faith in oneself	211
CHAPTER FIVE	215
The Mother who showers Her blessings	215
Mother drinks poisoned milk	219
Mother's real form	221
Surrendering to God	223
No time for sadhana	225
Mother in Ernakulam	228
Let dharma begin at a young age	229
Retarded children – whose karma causes their disability?	234
Advice to the brahmacharis	235
To be fit for realization	238
Mother's true nature	241
Rules for doing service	242
Monday, November 4, 1985	244
Vedanta – the true and the false	245
Mother's bhakti bhava	247
Brahma muhurta	249
Mother recounts old stories	252
GLOSSARY	258

FOREWORD

Rare indeed are the mahatmas (great souls) endowed with the vision of seeing the entire universe within the Atman (Self), and the Atman within the universe. Even if they are recognized, they may not be inclined to communicate with us or counsel us, immersed as they are in the eternal silence of the Self. Therefore, it is our great fortune when a fully realized mahatma is ready to advise and discipline us with the tender love of a mother, and the inexplicable compassion of a guru. Throughout the world today, the darshan and the nectarous words of Sri Mata Amritanandamayi Devi are effecting transformations in the lives of hundreds of thousands of people. This book, though incomplete, is a precious collection of conversations between the Holy Mother and Her disciples, devotees, and inquiring visitors during the period from June 1985 to September 1986.

The wisdom of the mahatmas, who have come with the mission of uplifting the world, has both immediate and eternal meaning. Even though they elucidate values that are everlasting, they are attuned to the call of the times in which they live, and their words are in response to the heartbeat of their listeners.

Mother speaks Her immortal words, which transform society, at a time when man has lost his traditional values, nobler sentiments, and peace of mind in the frenzied attempt to reinforce the outer world of sensory pleasures, power, and prestige. Man's senseless pursuit of these distractions, while he remains oblivious of his own Self, has cost him the harmony and graciousness of his life. Lack of faith, fear, and a sense of competition has destroyed personal ties and family relations. Love has become no more than a mirage in a culture of excessive consumerism.

Selfless love of God gives way to a form of devotion that is driven entirely by desires. Man gives undue importance to an intellect that seeks the yield of immediate profit, while discarding the lasting glory promised by true wisdom. Lofty spiritual principles and noble experiences do not shine in the lives of the people, but are confined to mere words. It is at such a juncture that Mother speaks to us in a language of untainted devotion, a language of the heart, of wisdom, and of the love that is Her entire life. Her ambrosial words have both an immediate and eternal relevance.

The wisdom of Mother, who has personally listened to countless problems confided by hundreds of thousands of people, shows Her deep insight into the human condition. She recognizes their needs and descends to the level of the rationalist, the believer, the scientist, the ordinary man, the housewife, the businessman, the scholar, and the illiterate—man, woman, or child—and gives each one the appropriate answer, befitting their requirements.

Mother points at Her own life and declares, "As I see everything as the Truth, or Brahman, I bow to that Truth; I bow to my Self. I serve everyone, seeing them as the Self." She accepts advaita (non-duality) as the ultimate truth; yet the path that She commonly prescribes is a harmonious blend of mantra japa, meditation on a divine form, devotional singing, archana, satsang, and selfless service to the world.

Her advice is not just theoretical, but highly practical and rooted in daily living. Her instructions shed light on the need for spiritual training and sadhana (spiritual practice) in the life of the individual and in society, the role of selfless service in the search for the Self, the importance of sincere prayer with devotion, and pure love. She also addresses issues concerning the code of conduct for the householder, the problems of daily life, the dharma of the relationship between man and woman, and practical guidelines for spiritual seekers, sometimes offering riddles of a philosophical nature.

We hear Her exhorting Her children to follow spirituality in their lives, to give up luxuries, to eliminate bad habits, and to serve those who suffer: "Children, God-realization is the real aim of life." Spirituality is not blind faith; it is the ideal that eliminates darkness. It is the principle that teaches us to face any adverse circumstance or obstacle with a smile. It is a teaching for the mind. Mother points out that we can effectively utilize all other learning only if we acquire this knowledge.

Mother's infinite wisdom emerges as words of comfort to those seeking solace from the problems of life, as answers to questions posed by those who are inquisitive about spirituality, and as instructions given from time to time to Her disciples. She gives each answer according to the nature and circumstances of the questioner. Even when the questioner is unable to express his ideas fully, Mother, who knows the language of the heart, gives the appropriate answer. An answer from

Mother, even before a doubt in the mind is expressed, is a common experience of those who come to Her.

In answer to a question explicitly put to Her by one person, it is Her practice to often include advice for a silent listener as well. Only the silent individual will understand that this was an answer for him. When one studies Mother's teachings, these special qualities should be kept in mind.

The words of a mahatma have many levels of meaning. We should absorb the meaning that is most appropriate for us. A well-known story in the Upanishads narrates that when Lord Brahma uttered the word 'da,' the demons interpreted it as advice to show compassion (daya), the humans as a call to give (dana), and the celestials as an injunction to practice restraint (dama).

Sweet is the experience of listening to Mother, and watching Her speak with vivid expressions and gestures, in a language that is simple, and at the same time, embellished with extremely appropriate stories and analogies drawn from life around Her. The love that shines in Mother's eyes, Her radiant, compassionate face, remain alive in the mirror of the listeners' mind as objects of meditation.

There is no scarcity of spiritual literature today, yet the sad fact remains that the highest ideals are confined to peoples' tongues, but are not found in their lives. Mother, however, speaks on the basis of Her daily life. She never gives advice that She Herself does not demonstrate in Her own life. She frequently reminds us that spiritual principles and mantras are not meant to remain on our lips, but are to be translated into our lives as well. The secret behind the deep spiritual principles flowing in a continuous stream from Mother, who has not studied the scriptures or taken instruction from a guru, is nothing but Her direct experience of the Self.

The lives of the mahatmas form the very foundation of the scriptures. Mother's sayings such as, "The whole world belongs to the one who knows Reality," "Kindness towards the poor is our duty to God," "If you take refuge in God, He will bring what you need when you need it," are mirrors of Her own life. In each of Her movements, there is the dance of compassion for the whole world, and love for God. Indeed, this unity of thought, word, and deed in Mother's life is the basis of Her statement that Her children do not need to study any other scripture if they analyze and study Her own life carefully. Mother shines in the midst of society as a living embodiment of Vedanta.

The mahatmas who sanctify the world through their presence are tirthas, holy places of pilgrimage, on the move. As regular pilgrimages and temple worship purify our minds when practiced for many years, so a single darshan, touch, or word from a mahatma sanctifies us and deposits in us seeds of exalted samskara.

The words of the mahatmas are not mere sounds. The mahatmas shower their grace along with their words. Their words are bound to awaken Consciousness, even in someone who listens without understanding their meaning. When these words appear in the form of a book, their study becomes the greatest satsang and meditation. Mahatmas like Mother, who have experienced Reality, transcend time and space. Reading or hearing Mother's immortal words enables us to maintain an unseen inner bond with Her and to become fit to receive Her blessings. That is the real greatness of the study of such books.

We humbly offer this collection of Mother's immortal words to the readers, with the prayer that it may inspire them to emulate the lofty spiritual ideals that shine throughout Her life, and to progress on the path of the ultimate Truth.

– The publishers

CHAPTER ONE

Monday, June 3, 1985

It is dawn. One can hear the sweet notes of the *tambura* from Mother's room. The tambura was given to Her by a devotee. Lately, She plays it for some time in the morning. Mother picks up the tambura only after touching it with reverence and bowing to it. She bows to it again while putting it down. To Mother, everything is a form of God. She often says that we should consider all musical instruments as forms of Devi Saraswati. During *bhajans*, one cannot tell when She puts down the bells She has been playing as She puts them down with such reverence and attention.

The Mother who never rests

Mother came to the darshan hut after nine in the morning. There were several devotees waiting for Her there.

Mother: "Children, have you been here for long?"

One devotee: "Just a short while. We were lucky today. We were able to hear Amma play the tambura."

Mother: "Amma lost track of time playing it. She did not have time to sleep after the *Bhava Darshan* last night. There were many letters to read and by the time they were all read, it was morning. Gayatri pressed Her several times to go to bed.

Amma kept saying, 'After one more.' But seeing the next letter, Amma could not resist opening and reading it. She could feel the sorrow of those children piercing Her own heart. Many of the children do not even expect a reply. All they want is Mother to read about their grief. How can Amma ignore that prayer? When their sorrow comes to mind, She would forget Her own difficulties completely. By the time She read all the letters, it was morning. She did not go to bed. After Her bath, Amma felt She needed some solitude. That is when She started playing the tambura. Its sound makes Amma lose Her mind. She does not feel the passage of time when She plays it. It was when the clock struck nine that you children came to mind, so Amma came here immediately!"

There is nothing unusual about Mother's routine today. Most days are like this. She has no time to eat or sleep. On many nights, it would be very late when She returned to Her room after the Bhava Darshan. Then She would start reading the letters. There are many letters every day. Most of them tell stories filled with tears, and Amma does not go to bed before reading them all. On some days She has a little time at noon to read the letters. Where does She find time to rest as She pays attention to the problems of Her children numbering in the hundreds of thousands? Only on very rare occasions will She get more than two hours of sleep. There is no sleep at all on some days, yet when She remembers that Her devotees are waiting for Her, She would forget everything and come running down. By then, all fatigue would be gone from Her face.

Advice to householders

A young woman holding an infant in her hand approached Mother and prostrated. Soiled clothes, hair in disarray, her face was stricken with grief.

Mother: "Are you going today, daughter?"

Woman: "Yes, Amma! I have been away from home for three days already."

She put her head on Mother's chest and started sobbing. Mother raised her face and wiped her tears, saying, "Don't worry daughter, everything will be all right."

The woman prostrated in front of Amma again and went out.

A devotee: "I know that young woman. She has changed so much."

Mother: "Her husband had a good job. He fell into some bad company, and started drinking. Soon he ran short of cash and asked for her jewelry to pay for his drinking. When she hesitated, he began beating her. Out of fear, she surrendered it all in the end. He sold it and spent all the money on drink. He would come home drunk every night and pull her down by her hair and beat her up. With all the beating, look at her shape now! A few days ago there was a fight for the little gold chain around the baby's neck and she was beaten up very badly. She picked up the child and came here. What a happy family it was in the beginning! Can any good come from intoxicants? Health, wealth, peace at home - all are lost."

Another woman: "One of our neighbors drinks. Recently, he came home drunk one day, picked up his daughter who was only a year-and-a-half old, and threw her violently. What kind of a mind is that! His wife is in sad shape with all the beating she takes."

Mother: "Children, when alcohol takes away the senses, a man is not able to recognize even his wife and children. He may come home after getting beaten up already in a senseless fight with someone. What kind of happiness does one get from these things?

"One just imagines that one gets pleasure from these things. Does happiness reside in cigarettes or alcohol or drugs? There are people who smoke away several hundred rupees per month. That money is enough for a child's education. Intoxicants may help one forget everything for just a short while. But in reality, the body loses its vitality and the person faces ruin; failing health leads to untimely death. Those who should be of benefit to the family and country end up destroying themselves and harming others, instead."

Devotee: "Amma, why do these people destroy themselves knowingly?"

Mother: "Children, it is a man's selfish search for pleasure that leads him to indulge in smoking and drinking. He thinks that all this mean happiness. We should explain spiritual principles to him. For that, each of us should be ready to live according to those principles. Then others will emulate us. They will also become big-hearted. Selfishness will fall away.

"We see people who spend thousands on excessive comfort and pomp. At the same time, their neighbor may be starving. A girl's wedding is called off because the parents are unable to give a thousand rupees as dowry. In another family, a married daughter has been sent back home, because she was not given a big enough share of her father's wealth. Their neighbor, meanwhile, is spending millions on the marriage of their daughter. Those who have the means but are not willing to help others in need do the greatest harm to society. They are also betraying their own souls."

Leading a spiritual life to purify one's conduct

Mother's face became serious. She said in a firm voice, "Children, such a selfish mind can be made generous only through spiritual thoughts. All of us are the same Self; all are the children of the same mother - the Mother of the Universe. We all breathe the same air. When I was born, I had no name or caste; caste and religion came much later. Therefore, my duty is to break down those barriers and love everyone as brothers and sisters; I can find true happiness in life only through loving and helping others. True worship of God is rendering help to those who are suffering. We should live immersed in such thoughts. They will broaden our point of view. When we grasp these principles, there will be a real change in our character. We will be full of compassion.

"Nowadays, most people have only the attitude of 'I' and 'mine.' They think only of their own happiness and that of their family. That is death; it ruins themselves and society. Children, we should explain to such people, 'This is not how you should live! You are not little ponds where water stagnates and gets dirtier with time; you are rivers that should flow for the benefit of the world. You are not meant to suffer; you are meant to experience bliss!'

"By flowing into a river, the water in the pond gets cleaner; by flowing into a gutter it only gets dirtier. The gutter is the selfish attitude of 'I and mine.' The river is God. Let us take refuge in God, children. We will gain whether we win or lose. By taking refuge in God, we get peace of mind and happiness. Peace and prosperity grow within the family and in the world."

Mother looks at a devotee sitting near Her and says, "When this son first came to see Amma, he was totally drunk and was not conscious at all; some others supported him and brought him in." (She laughs.)

Devotee: "After seeing Amma I haven't taken a drink. Some of my friends also quit drinking when they saw that I had given up the habit. Now I dislike even hearing about alcohol."

Mother: "Son, when you changed for the better, didn't some others also change at the same time? Didn't that bring peace to their families as well?

"Children, we take birth and we create our own children; but beyond this, what are we doing for the good of the world? It is true that we are taking care of our wives and children. But is that our only duty? How can we get peace just from that? Are we contented when death comes? As we live without knowing the principles of a righteous life, we not only experience sorrow ourselves, but give sorrow to others as well. We also give life to some children who undergo pain themselves. Isn't this our life today?"

A devotee: "Is Amma saying that we should not have wives and children?"

Mother: "No, Amma is not saying that. What She is saying is that we should learn to gain peace in this life instead of spending this lifetime in an animal-like existence. Instead of going after pleasures, understand the goal of life and live for that. Lead a simple life. Give to others what is left after meeting one's own needs. Live without causing harm to others. Teach others these principles also. What we give the world should be that kind of good culture. Let us make our own hearts good and thus make others good as well. That is what we need. If we do this we will always feel peace and contentment within us, even if we lack external comforts.

"Even if we cannot render help to others, at least do not cause them any harm; that itself is a great service. But that is not enough. Try to be engaged in some work that will benefit others. Limit everything to what is really needed; do not undertake anything that is not essential. Food, thought, sleep and talk, all should be limited to the essential. If we live according to such a discipline, there will be only good thoughts in the mind. Such people will not pollute the atmosphere; they will sanctify it instead. We should consider such people as role models."

The faces of the devotees reflected that they were moved deeply by Mother's advice for the welfare of the individual and society. They saw that She was giving Her devotees very clear guidance on how to conduct the rest of their lives. They prostrated in front of Amma with the feeling of fulfillment from having spent some priceless moments in Her company.

Monday, June 10, 1985

It was ten in the morning. Some *brahmacharis* (celibate students) and devotees were sitting near Mother in front of the *kalari*, the old temple. On the right side of the kalari was the building that housed the office, library, kitchen and dining room. At the back of the building there were also three small rooms for the brahmacharis. Mother's family lived in this house until they moved to a new building. On the left side of the kalari were the Vedanta school, other huts, Mother's room and the meditation hall.

The Guru's instructions

Mother: "Amma severely scolded one of Her sons today." She was referring to one of the brahmacharis.

Devotee: "Why, Amma?"

Mother: "He went to Kollam the other day to get the car repaired. Before he left, Amma had told him to return on the same day whether or not the repair was done. But he stayed there overnight since the car was not ready. When he came back the next day, Amma scolded him. Yesterday he went back without telling Her or even leaving Her a note. Today Amma rebuked him for everything. Amma is unhappy when She has to take Her children to task. But the quality of a spiritual seeker is shown by the way he obeys instructions. What can Mother do? She appears very cruel towards Her children at times.

"Some patients don't allow the doctor to give them injections because they are afraid it will hurt them. But the doctor knows that they will not be cured without the injections, so he gives the injections even if he has to use force to restrain the patients while doing so. If, out of kindness, he refrains from giving injections, the patient may die. The treatment is unavoidable for the cure. Similarly, a real guru is one who insists that the disciple obey him, and uses his will to get compliance.

This is necessary for the disciple to reach his goal. It is the duty of the guru to make the disciple do what is needed. A blacksmith heats up a piece of iron in the furnace and beats on it repeatedly, not out of cruelty, but only for giving it the desired shape. Someone may cut paper up into many pieces, only to make a beautiful flower out of it. Similarly, the guru reprimands and disciplines the disciple, only to reveal the nature of the Self to him. Every punishment that he gives shows his great compassion towards the disciple. The disciple should acquire humility, an attitude of surrender and an attitude that he is the servant of the guru; only then the guru would shower his grace on him and raise him to the guru's own world. The disciple should have the attitude, 'I am nothing; you are everything; I am only your instrument.'

"Everything except our sense of ego belongs to God. Only the ego is ours and it is not easily removed. Only through obedience to the guru can we wipe out the ego. When we follow the guru's instructions and bend to his will, the ego will disappear due to his grace.

"A log that floats down the river moves with the flow of the river. Similarly, the disciple should move in accordance with the guru's wish, with an attitude of surrender that 'you are everything.' This is the only way to remove the ego. What power do we possess that we can call 'our will'? Someone says from the top of the stairs, 'I am coming down now,' but he falls down dead after walking down just ten steps. Aren't there countless instances like that? If it were 'our will,' wouldn't he come all the way down as he said? But was he able to do that? Therefore we have to see that everything is the Lord's will."

Mother joined Her hands and prayed aloud, "O Devi, at

least from now on, kindly do not make me scold my children! Give them intelligence and discrimination! Give them your blessings!" Amma stayed in that pose for a few moments. Those around Her also joined their hands, closed their eyes and prayed.

Tuesday, June 11, 1985

Abode of compassion

It was four in the afternoon. Mother came down to the hut to give darshan. There was a snake on one side of the hut. The devotees and brahmacharis were trying to get rid of it. Mother approached them.

"Children, don't hurt it! Just throw some sand at it." The snake moved away slowly, as if it heard Amma's words. "Many prostrations to the Devi who resides in all beings in the form of compassion," as the scriptures say!

Mother sat down in the hut to give darshan. The devotees came one by one and prostrated, surrendering their burdens at Her feet. They submitted to Her ears their desires and the problems that gnawed away their peace of mind. Some burst into tears the moment they saw Mother. Those who came to Her struggling under the torment of life, returned with contented and peaceful minds.

When all the devotees departed, the brahmacharis gathered around Mother.

A brahmachari: "Amma did not discuss anything spiritual today."

Mother: "Son, all the people sitting here were full of

suffering. What a hungry child needs is not a discourse on Vedanta or on the principles of spirituality. First let us reduce the sorrow of these people. Then we can talk about spirituality. It is difficult for them to absorb anything like that now.

"But those who are thirsting for God would not like to talk about anything but God, even when great sorrow befalls them. They will be even-minded in sorrow and happiness. When happiness comes, they don't lose their minds reveling in it, nor do they collapse in times of grief. They accept both as the will of the Lord. They accept both as His blessing.

"If a thorn pricks your foot when you walk, you will take your steps more carefully and you will escape falling into a ditch that may be just ahead. God gives us sorrow to save us. True believers will cling to the feet of the Lord even in sorrow. In their prayers, they will never ask for happiness. They will never think of selfish gains. But when somebody who suffers comes to us, we should give him solace. We should find time to speak a few comforting words. Very few people do that."

Mother sees the sorrow of others as Her own. She finds delight in taking on the burdens of others. Amma is the sacrificial fire into which everyone's *prarabdha* (past actions bearing fruit) is offered. She is the beacon of hope for all those who suffer.

Amma came out of the temple after the Bhava Darshan. Everyone gathered around Her. Most of the devotees were planning to leave on the morning bus. They crowded around Amma anxiously, to prostrate to Her once more and get Her blessings before leaving. However, one young man did not approach Her. He sat alone on the porch of the meditation room, away from the crowd. A brahmachari asked him, "Aren't you going to Amma?"

Young Man: "No."

Br: "When everyone is anxious to be near Amma and talk to her, why are you sitting here alone?"

Young Man: "I have also been like them. Normally, I wait outside the kalari, wanting to be the first to prostrate to Amma as She comes out. But today my mind doesn't allow me to go near Her at all. I am such a sinner."

Br: "I don't believe that. You are imagining something. What error did you commit that won't let you go near Amma now?"

Young man: "I live in Kollam. I drank regularly for a few years. This led me to fight with my wife. I sent her to her parents' home. My family and neighbors hated me. I didn't have a friend in the world. Finally I decided to end my life. It is then that I had the immense good fortune to have Amma's darshan. That was a turning point in my life. After my first darshan, I stopped drinking completely. There was a great change in my behavior. People changed their opinion of me. But I drank again today. I went into a liquor shop at the insistence of some friends. We had gone to a wedding. On the way back, my friends wanted to drink. They pressed me to join them, and I yielded. But later, I couldn't bear my sense of guilt. I came here immediately. Earlier, I had no feeling of guilt, however much I drank. But now it is different. (*His voice cracking*) Now I find it hard to even look at Amma's face."

Br: "This remorse itself is atonement for your mistake. Don't worry. Tell Amma everything. All your worries will be over."

CHAPTER 1

Young Man: "I need only to bow down in front of Her. All my uneasiness will be gone. That has been my experience. That is not what is bothering me now. My friends will not leave me alone if I remain at home. Therefore I would like to stay here for a few days. But I don't have the courage to ask Amma. I feel so weak when I think that I have erred again in the eyes of my Amma who showers more love on me than the mother who gave birth to me."

His eyes were full of tears. The brahmachari did not have the words needed to console the young man. But there was someone there who understood the throbbing pain in his heavy heart.

After showing the other devotees where to sleep, Mother came over to the young man. He got up immediately and stood reverently with joined hands. Amma held both his hands in Hers and asked, "Are you so weak, my son?"

Tears flowed down his cheeks. Wiping them, Amma continued, "Son, stop worrying. Why feel sorry about what is past? Don't go with those people when they call you again, that is all.

"Once, a temple and a liquor shop both kept parrots as pets. While the temple parrot chanted Vedic mantras, the liquor shop parrot mouthed obscenities. Son, one's conduct is determined by the company one keeps. If we sit in a room with the TV on, we will end up looking at it. If we don't want to look at it, we have to turn it off or go to another room. If we associate with bad people, we will retain their habits. So we have to take special care not to fall into such company. Son, if you have some problem on your mind, you can come to Amma. Amma is here for you. Stay here for a few days. Get some books from the library to read."

Amma turned to the brahmachari. "Make arrangements for this son to stay upstairs in the house on the north side."

When the young man heard these loving words from the Mother who knew every thought in his mind, he could not control himself. He burst into tears again.

Wiping the streaming tears of remorse from his face with Her loving hands, Amma consoled him, "Son, go to bed now. Amma will talk to you tomorrow."

After sending the young man away with the brahmachari, Mother went to the coconut grove in front of the ashram, accompanied by a female devotee who had waited for a long time for a chance to talk to Her in private. By the time Amma went to Her, it was past three in the morning.

Wednesday, June 12, 1985

Bhakti yoga

Mother came to the kalari, accompanied by three or four brahmacharis and some householder devotees who were at the ashram for the first time. Amma was talking to them about the importance of having pure devotion to God.

Mother: "Amma's prayer used to be this: 'O Devi, I only want a heart to love You; it is all right if You don't give me Your darshan, just give me a heart that loves everyone! It is all right if You don't love me; but please let me have love for You!' Someone who is full of love for God is like someone suffering from fever. He won't have any taste for food. He won't savor salty or sour dishes; even sweet dishes would taste bitter to him. He wouldn't be interested in food at all. But it is very unusual for a seeker to feel such love in the beginning. Therefore, in the beginning, one should exercise control of various habits with *shraddha* (attention), especially in the matter of food. If the mind wanders off to external things, one should bring it back, again and again, to the thought of God. Not a single moment should be wasted."

A devotee: "Amma, I don't waste any time. Either I come here to be near you, or I go to a temple. Isn't that all I can do?"

Mother: "Coming here and going to temples are all fine, but the aim must be to purify the mind. If we can't make our minds pure, everything is a waste. Don't think that we can get peace without making our mind and our actions pure. We should remember this when we go to see Mahatmas or visit temples. We should have an attitude of surrender. Yet these days, most people worry about reserving a room in the lodge even before they leave home; the moment they start the trip, they begin talking about family and neighbors. This doesn't stop even when they return home. God is just forgotten in the middle of all this. We may visit any number of Mahatmas or temples, or make any number of offerings, but only through our sadhana will we receive some benefit. Our hearts must be tuned to God. Just visiting Tirupati or Kashi (places of pilgrimage in India) does not bring liberation. One may not gain much spiritually or materially just by bathing and circumambulating the temples in those places. If one could get liberation by going to Tirupati, all the businessmen there would be liberated by now, wouldn't they?

"Don't forget God's name wherever you go! Look at the

'metal'[1] that is mixed with concrete for fixing up the roads. Only if the metal is clean, will the concrete set properly. In the same way, only if we purify our hearts through japa can we install God inside. For purifying the mind, there is no better way than chanting the Divine Name.

"Even if they transmit TV programs from the studio, we can only see them at home if we turn the television set on. Isn't it useless to blame others if you can't see anything on the TV because you didn't turn it on? God's grace flows to us always. But to benefit from it, we have to be tuned to His world. What good is it to stay inside with all the doors closed, and complain that it is all dark, when the sun is shining brightly outside? If we just open the doors of our hearts, we can receive the grace that the Lord is showering constantly. God showers his compassion on us always. How we benefit from it depends on how we receive it within us.

"Children, until we tune ourselves to the world of God, we produce only the jarring notes of ignorance, not divine music. We have to put up with their lack of quality. There is no use in blaming others for it.

"We are willing to wait for a bus, however long it takes. We don't mind spending the whole day at the courthouse pursuing some legal goal or other. But we have no patience when we visit a Mahatma or go to a temple. When you go to the ashram or the temple, spend some time there, remembering God with devotion. Chant the Divine Name and meditate for awhile, or be engaged in some selfless work. Only then, will there be some benefit from the visit."

---

[1] Road metal: Broken pieces of stone used in repairing roads.

The importance of the right attitude

Mother continued: "If our minds are pure, if we do everything remembering God, His grace will be on us even if we don't go to temples or anywhere. On the other hand, countless trips to the temple won't do us any good if we cannot stop being selfish or hating others.

"There were two women who were neighbors. One was a devotee of God and the other a prostitute. The devotee would tell her neighbor, 'What you are doing is very sinful. It will only lead you to hell.' The prostitute remembered this always. She used to shed tears every day, thinking, 'What a sinner I am! I have no other livelihood, therefore I am doing this. O God, please pardon me! At least in my next birth, let me have the chance to pray to you and worship you daily as my friend is doing! Please forgive my mistakes!'

"The other woman kept thinking about the prostitute and her way of life with disapproval, even when she was in the temple. Finally both women died. Attendants from heaven and hell arrived. The prostitute was about to be taken to heaven and her friend to hell. The pious woman could not bear this at all. She asked the divine attendants, 'You are taking to heaven someone who sold her body throughout her life; I worshipped and prayed at the temple daily, yet you are taking me to hell. What kind of justice is this? You must be mistaken.'

The heavenly attendants replied, 'We are not mistaken. Even when you visited the temple and did *puja* (ceremonial worship), your thoughts were about the bad actions of your friend. On the other hand, even though your friend was a prostitute, she did not identify with her work; her thoughts were on God. She did not pass a single day without feeling remorse about her errors and asking God for forgiveness. Even though she was forced to earn her living as a prostitute, she was a true devotee. That is why she is going to heaven.'"

For spiritual seekers

The evening bhajan was over. Mother came out and lay down on the sand between the kalari and the meditation room. The dinner bell rang and Amma asked the devotees to go and eat. They left one by one. Only one or two brahmacharis stayed back, meditating in Amma's presence.

All the devotees came back after dinner and sat around Mother. One woman placed Amma's feet in her lap and started rubbing them.

Mother: "Did you eat, children?"

A devotee: "Yes, Amma, all of us ate."

Mother: "You would have tasty dishes at home. There is nothing here. You must not have eaten enough."

Another devotee: "We all filled ourselves, Amma. We may have a lot of dishes at home, but nothing tastes as good as what we get here."

Mother (laughing): "Son, you are just saying that out of love for Amma!" Everybody laughs.

A devotee: "Amma, I have a doubt."

Mother: "Children, you can ask Amma anything."

Devotee: "I heard you tell a brahmachari the other day that we should take a vow of *ahimsa* (non-violence). We should not be angry with anyone. Even if someone is angry with us, we should see God in them and show love towards them. Isn't this very hard to practice?"

Mother: "Son, the important thing is not whether we are totally successful in this, but whether we have tried sincerely or not. Those who have dedicated their lives to spirituality should be ready for some sacrifices. Their life is already set on this path. If someone opposes them, they should treat it as an opportunity created by God to eliminate their sense of ego. They should not fight back under the spell of the ego. A *sadhak* (spiritual aspirant) can grow only by seeing God in everyone and showing love."

A devotee: "Amma, I have given up many things for the sake of God, but I don't find peace."

Mother: "Son, all of us talk about the sacrifices we have made. But what do we really have that we can give up? What do we have that is our own? What we consider ours today will not be ours tomorrow. Everything belongs to God. We are able to enjoy things only through His grace. If there is anything that is our own, it is our desire and our anger. That is what we need to renounce. Even though we renounce many things now, we don't give up our attachment to them. That is the reason for our sorrow. True renunciation happens only when we are convinced in our hearts that relatives, wealth, position or fame will not give lasting peace. What does the *Gita* (Bhagavad Gita - a scripture) teach? Isn't it to act without attachment?"

The danger of wealth

Amma started telling a story. "Once there was a rich man. One day some of his friends came to see him. They saw a servant outside the house and asked him where his master was. After searching inside, the servant came back and told them that his master was counting pebbles. 'Such a rich man counting pebbles?' wondered the guests among themselves.

"When the rich man appeared a little later, they asked him about this. He replied, 'I was counting money. Is my servant so dumb as to think I was counting pebbles? Anyway, I am sorry for the confusion.'

"A few days later another friend came to see the rich man. He asked the servant to find his master. The servant reported, after looking inside, 'He is loving his enemy.' The rich man was in fact counting his money and putting it away in his safe. He felt that the servant had deliberately insulted him and was enraged by the impudence. He beat the servant up and expelled him. He gave the departing servant a doll and said, 'If you see anyone more foolish than yourself, give him this doll!' The servant departed silently.

"Some months passed. One night the rich man's house was robbed. The robbers took all the wealth. When the rich man tried to stop them, they threw him down from the upper floor of the house and escaped with everything. The next morning, relatives found the rich man lying on the ground in front of the house. He was unable to get up. Many treatments were tried, but his health could not be restored. All his wealth was gone, and because of that, his wife and children also left him. He was in pain. There was no one to look after him. He did not have any food at home. He ate whatever his neighbors gave him.

"His old servant heard about his troubles and came to see him. He had the old doll with him. As soon as he arrived, he offered the doll to his master. His master asked him, 'Why are you aggravating my wounds?'

"The servant replied, 'At least by now, you must have understood the meaning of what I said. Is the money you had amassed worth as much as even a pebble to you now? Didn't your wealth in fact turn out to be your enemy? Your wealth is what brought you to this state. Didn't you lose everything because of your wealth? Who is more foolish than you who made such wealth the object of love? Those who loved you till now, really loved your money, not you. When your money was gone, you were as good as dead in their eyes. Now no one loves you. Realize, at least now, that God is your only lasting friend. Call for his help!'

"The servant began nursing his master with love. The rich man was full of repentance. 'I don't know what I will do now. My life has been useless. I thought that my wife and children and my wealth will be here forever, and I lived for them. I didn't remember God even for a moment. But now everything is gone. Those who bowed their heads in front of me with respect don't even glance at me now. They spit at me in contempt.'

"The servant consoled him, 'Don't think that you have no one to look after you. The Lord is there.' He stayed with his old master and nursed him."

Mother stopped. One man who was sitting at the back of the group of devotees started weeping loudly. This was his first visit to Amma. He was crying bitterly, unable to control his grief. Amma called him near and consoled him.

Still sobbing, the man said, "Amma, what you just narrated is my own story. All my money is gone. My wife and children hate me. My only solace is my old servant."

Mother said, wiping his tears, "What is gone is gone, my son! Don't grieve over that. God is the only lasting thing. Everything else will be gone today or tomorrow. It is enough if you live with that thought in your mind. Don't worry!"

Mother asked Br. Balagopal[2], sitting nearby, to sing the song, *'Manasse nin svantamayi.'* He sang:

> *Remember, O mind, this supreme truth:*
> *Nobody is your own!*
>
> *Because of doing meaningless actions,*
> *You are wandering in the ocean of this world.*
>
> *Even though people honor you,*
> *Calling you, "Lord, Lord,"*
> *It will be only for a short time.*
>
> *Your body, which has been honored for so long,*
> *Must be cast off when life departs.*
>
> *The sweetheart for whom you have been struggling*
> *All this time, not even caring for your life,*
> *Even she will be frightened by your dead body*
> *And will not accompany you.*
>
> *Trapped in the subtle snare of Maya as you are,*
> *Do not forget the sacred name*
> *Of the Divine Mother.*

---

[2] Now Swami Amritaswarupananda.

*The Lord will attract devotion-soaked souls
Like a magnet attracts iron.
Position, prestige and wealth are impermanent,
The only Reality is the universal Mother.*

*Renouncing all desires,
Let us dance in that bliss
Singing the name of Mother Kali.*

Wednesday, June 19, 1985

Mother of the Universe

A young man with long hair and a beard came to the Ashram. He approached a brahmachari and introduced himself as a reporter from a newspaper. "We have heard several good and bad things about Amma," he said, "I have come to find out what is really going on in this Ashram. I talked to one or two residents. But there is one thing I don't understand at all."

Br: "What is that?"

Reporter: "How can educated people like you believe blindly in a human God?"

Br: "What do you mean by God? Do you mean a being with four arms, wearing a crown, and sitting in a heaven beyond the sky?"

Reporter: "No. Each one has his own concept of God. Generally we imagine God as the embodiment of all the qualities that we consider sublime."

Br: "Then what is wrong in worshipping as divine an individual in whom we see all those divine qualities? If we don't accept that, we are saying that God is limited to the idols that man sculpts out of stone, installs in a temple and worships.

"The spiritual texts of India declare that a human being, an individual soul (*jivatman*) is really not different from God, and that he understands his divinity when his ego (the sense that he is limited) is destroyed through constant practice. If the all-pervading Supreme can manifest through an idol, why can't it shine through an individual?"

The reporter had no answer.

The brahmachari continued, "In Amma we see all the qualities that the scriptures attribute to God, such as love, compassion, selflessness, forgiveness and equal treatment of all. Therefore, some of us see Her as the Mother of the Universe. Others see Her as the loving Mother who was with us in all our births. Some others consider Her as the Guru who awakens the knowledge of the Self. She Herself does not claim to be God or Guru or to be anything at all. If you want fish from the ocean you get fish, but if you want pearls, you get them too. Similarly, there is everything in Amma. If we put forth the effort, we can get what we want.

"The message of the Upanishads is that each of us is the essence of the Supreme. Weren't Rama and Krishna and Buddha all on this earth in human form at one time? If we can worship them, why can't we worship someone who shows all of their infinite, glorious qualities, while She is in human form, in our midst?"

Reporter: "Isn't it enough to think of Her as guru? Why turn Her into God?"

Br: "That is fine! But the scriptures say that guru is none

other than God in human form! In a way, our tradition places guru even higher than God."

By this time, Amma had arrived in the hut and started giving darshan to the devotees. The brahmachari invited the reporter to go to Her, "Let us go in. You can put your questions directly to Amma."

The reporter took a seat near Mother. He watched with wonder as the devotees approached Amma one by one and She caressed and consoled each one with overflowing love.

When the reporter was introduced to Her, Amma laughed.

Mother: "Amma doesn't read newspapers or anything, my son! Most of the children here don't even see a paper."

Reporter: "I was asking a brahmachari here whether Amma was God."

Mother: "She is just a crazy woman! All these people call Her 'Amma' and so She calls them Her children!"

Most of the time Mother hides Her true self as She talks. Only someone who has acquired a measure of spiritual insight can appreciate Her innate nature even a little. Many people picture a guru as somebody who sits on a splendid throne, with a smile, always served by his disciples and showering blessings on all. But those who come to the Ashram will have to give up this idea. Someone who sees Amma for the first time will find in Her a person more normal than most normal people. She can be seen cleaning the front yard, cutting vegetables, cooking, showing the devotees to their rooms or carrying a load of sand. However, for someone who knows what the scriptures say, it is easy to recognize the true Mother. Her humility declares aloud Her greatness.

Once a brahmachari asked Mother, "With the attainment

of even the slightest *siddhi* (mystic power), most individuals would go around pretending to be Brahman, and accept many disciples. People put their trust in them. When this is happening everywhere, why does Amma deceive Her children, saying She is nothing?"

Mother gave the following answer: "The brahmacharis living here today are meant to go out into the world tomorrow. They are to become role models for the world. Here they learn from every word and every action of Mother. If there is even a trace of ego in Her words and actions, it will become tenfold in each of them. They will think, 'If Amma can do that, why can't I?' And that will do harm to the world.

"Do you children know how hard it is for Amma to live at your level? A father tries hard to walk with his little baby, taking tiny steps. He does not do it for his own sake. Only if he takes small steps, can the child keep up with him. This role that Amma is taking on is not for Her; it is for all of you. Just for your growth. When a child has jaundice, a loving mother will avoid cooking hot and salty dishes. She will hide all such foods, because the child may eat them if it finds them. Then it may get fever and may even die. For the sake of the child, the mother also eats bland food, without any spices. Even though she is not sick, she renounces her taste. In the same way, all of Amma's words and actions are for your good. At every step, She thinks of your growth. Only if the doctor is a nonsmoker will the patient accept his instruction to give up smoking. Only if the doctor doesn't drink, will the patient also be inspired to give up drinking. Amma does nothing for Herself. Everything is for the world. Everything is to help you advance."

The reporter asked Mother, "Amma, aren't you guiding the people here as their guru?"

Mother: "That depends on each person's attitude. Amma didn't have a guru; and She hasn't taken anyone as disciple, either. Amma only says that everything works according to the will of the Divine Mother."

Reporter: "I have a friend who is a great devotee of J. Krishnamurty."Mother: "Many children have come here who are his devotees. Western children like him particularly."

Reporter: "Krishnamurty doesn't take any disciples. No one resides with him. We can go near him. We can talk to him. It is believed that we get what we want just from the conversation. His very presence is an inspiration. He is very jolly. There is no aura of a guru around him."

Mother: "But, his very statement that you don't need a guru is a teaching, isn't it? And when someone is near him listening , don't we have a guru and a disciple there?"

Reporter: "He doesn't give advice or instructions."

Mother: "But what about his speeches, son?"

Reporter: "They are just like conversations, very light in nature."

Mother: "No guru insists that others should obey him or live according to his words. But every word from a guru is advice. His life itself is his teaching. We listen to Krishnamurti's words. And when we follow those words, we come to know our real essence, right? That readiness to follow is nothing but discipleship. It nurtures humility and good conduct in us. Only the children who grow up following their parents' advice usually become good adults.

"Obeying our parents instills the sense of duty and right

conduct in us. Amma is not saying that Krishnamurty's method is wrong. He has read many books. He has gone to many wise people and learnt much from them. He has taught himself a lot. Only then he reached his present level. He understood that everything is within himself. But son, you haven't reached that state.

"Today, our attention is mainly in external things. We hardly ever look inward. When children are in school, their interest is mostly in playing. They study mainly out of fear of their parents. But when they begin to have an aim, to graduate with a high rank, to become an engineer, do they start studying without any prodding. Even though we have a spiritual goal, the mind slips away from it due to the pressure of *vasanas* (tendencies). To control such a mind, a *Satguru* (Self-realized Master) is essential. But after a certain stage, no help is needed. The guru within is awake then.

"The hymn that we once memorized may be forgotten in time, but if someone reminds us of the opening line, we will be able to recite the whole thing. Similarly, all wisdom is within us; the guru reminds us of it. He awakens what is dormant.

"Guru comes in, even in the statement that one doesn't need a guru. After all, someone had to tell us that we didn't need a guru. A guru is one who removes our ignorance. If one hasn't achieved a certain purity of mind, it is essential to spend some time under the guidance of a guru. Even if you have an innate talent in music, only after you practice under someone, are you able to display that talent fully.

"Ordinary gurus can only explain spiritual principles. But Satgurus, who have realized the Self, impart some of their spiritual power to the disciples. This enables the disciple to reach the goal more rapidly. Just as the tortoise makes the eggs hatch by the power of its thoughts, the Satguru's thoughts awaken the spiritual power in the disciple.

"Satsang and spiritual books have the power to turn our minds towards good thoughts. But those alone will not enable us to go forward in steady steps. Ordinary physicians will examine the patient and prescribe medicines. But if an operation is required, one has to see a surgeon. Likewise, to rid our minds of all the dirt and progress towards the ultimate goal, we have to take refuge in a guru."

Reporter: "Don't the scriptures say that everything is within us? Then what is the need for all this sadhana?"

Mother: "Although everything is within us, it is useless if we don't actually experience it. For that, sadhana is unavoidable. The *rishis* (seers) who gave us the *mahavakyas* (great sayings) such as 'I am Brahman,' 'Thou art That,' were individuals who had reached that plane of experience. Their way of life was so different from ours. They viewed every living thing as equal. They loved and served every being equally. In their eyes, nothing in the universe was separate from themselves. While they had the qualities of God, we have the qualities of a fly. A fly lives in dirt and excreta. Similarly, our minds can see only mistakes and defects in others. That has to change. We have to be able to see good in everything. Until we realize the truth through sadhana and contemplation, there is no sense in saying everything is already inside us.

"People who have studied the scriptures and Vedanta for forty or fifty years come here. Even they say they have no peace of mind. We can't get light by hanging a picture of a lamp on the wall. If we need to see anything, we have to turn the real light on. Learning from books and giving speeches will not be enough. To experience truth, one has to do sadhana, and discover the 'real I.' A guru's help is essential for that."

Reporter: "Is that the help Mother is giving here?"

Mother: "Amma does not do anything Herself. The *Paramatman* (Supreme Self) makes Her do everything! These people need Amma now. The seeker needs the guru. Why? Our minds are weak now. Little children like to poke their hands into fire. Their mother will tell them, 'Don't touch it, my son, it will burn your hand!' Someone has to tell that to the child to turn it away from the fire. That is all Amma is doing. Up to certain point, we need someone to point out our errors."

Reporter: "Isn't it slavery when one follows the guru blindly?

Mother: "My son, to know the Truth, we have to get rid of the 'I' sense. It is hard to achieve that just by doing sadhana ourselves. To eliminate the ego, it is essential to do spiritual practice under the guru's guidance. When we bow our heads in front of the guru, we are not bowing to that individual, but to the ideal in him. We do that so that we may also attain to his level.

"We can rise only through humility. The seed contains the tree within it. But if it is content to lie in the storeroom somewhere, it will be eaten by mice, that is all. Only by going under the soil, its true form will emerge. When you push the button down, the umbrella unfolds; it is then able to protect others from the rain.

"When we respected and obeyed our parents, our elders and teachers, we grew and gained knowledge. It nurtured good qualities and good behavior in us. In the same way, obedience to the guru elevates the disciple to a broader, higher plane.

"It is to become the king of kings later that the disciple takes the role of a servant now. We put a fence around a little mango tree, we nurture it and raise it - so we can get the sweet fruit later. One shows reverence to the guru and obeys him in order to reach the Truth that he represents.

"When we board the plane, they ask us to fasten our seat belts. It is not to show off their power over us. It is for our safety. In the same way, the guru asks the disciple to obey rules and practice restraint, only to elevate him. It is only to protect the disciple from the dangers that may befall him. The guru knows that the disciple's ego-driven impulses will cause danger to him and to others. The road is for the use of vehicles. But if you drive your car as you please, accidents are sure to happen. That is why we are asked to obey the rules of the road. Don't we obey the policeman who directs traffic at the intersections? We prevent many accidents by doing so.

"When our senses of 'I' and 'mine' are about to destroy us, we are saved by following the Satguru's advice. He gives us the training needed to avoid such circumstances later. The very nearness to the guru gives us strength.

"The guru is the embodiment of selflessness. We are able to learn what truth, dharma, renunciation, and love mean because gurus live in those qualities. The very life of those qualities is the guru. By obeying and emulating him, those qualities take root in us. Obedience to the guru is not slavery. The guru's aim is only the safety of the disciple. He truly shows us the path. A true guru will never see his disciple as his slave. He is filled with love for the disciple. He wants to see the disciple succeed even if it means hardship for himself. The true guru is indeed like your mother."

Mother's words dove deep into the listener's mind, uprooting doubts and planting the seeds of faith. The reporter took leave with the satisfaction of imbibing much that he had not known before.

Saturday, June 22, 1985

Meditation

Mother and the brahmacharis were sitting in the meditation room. Some householder devotees were also sitting nearby. A newly arrived brahmachari wanted to know more about meditation. He did not waste the chance to be with Mother in the morning.

Br: "Amma, what is meant by meditation?"

Mother: "Let us say we are going to make *payasam* (a sweet pudding made of rice). If someone asks us why we are pouring water into the pot, we say it is for payasam. But we are just taking water to be heated. Similarly, when we get the rice and the jaggery (unrefined brown sugar), we say those things are for payasam. In fact, the payasam is still to come. In the same way, when we sit with our eyes closed, we say we are meditating. Truly speaking, it is not meditation, it is a sadhana to reach true meditation. True meditation is a state of the mind, an experience. It cannot be described in words.

"Don't we talk about '*sadhakam*' in connection with singing? It just means practicing to sing. To sing well, one has to practice repeatedly and attain proficiency. In the same way, on the spiritual path, sadhana is practice and meditation is the state you reach as a result of it.

"Constant thought directed to God is meditation - like the flow of a river. You reach the state of meditation only by achieving true one-pointedness. In the beginning, one should purify the mind, make it one-pointed and dissolve it through japa and hymns, and then practice meditation.

"Without feeling love for God within, we cannot fasten our minds on Him. Once someone has that love, his mind will not stray again towards worldly things. To him, worldly pleasures are like dog's excreta. Little babies will pick up mud and dirt and put them in their mouths. Will they be tempted to do so, even a little bit, once they grow up and get some discrimination?"

The sorrows of worldly life

A brahmachari brought letters that had just arrived. Mother started reading them. She said to the devotees, as She was reading: "Just reading these, one can see all about life. Most of these are tales of suffering."

Br: "Are there no letters asking questions on spiritual matters?

Mother: "Yes, but most letters tell stories of sorrow. Like the letter that came the other day from a daughter. Her husband comes home drunk every day and beats her up. One day their two-year old child came between them. What is the difference between a child and an adult, to someone who is totally drunk? Just one kick and the baby's leg was broken. The leg is now in a cast. Even after this, the husband drinks just as much.

The wife has to take care of the baby and do everything else at home. She wrote for Amma's blessings so that her husband would stop drinking."

A devotee: "Amma, do you read all these letters yourself? There is a big bundle just from today's mail."

Mother: "When Amma thinks of their tears, how can She not read them all? She will write replies to some of them Herself. If there are a lot of letters, She will explain to someone what to write. It is hard to read and reply to all of them. Some letters fill ten or twelve sheets. Amma doesn't have time even to read them all. She would read letters almost until daybreak. She would have a letter in Her hands while She eats something. Often Amma dictates a reply while taking Her bath."

She gave the letters to a brahmachari, saying, "Put all these letters in Amma's room, son. Amma will read them later."

Details of sadhana

Mother asked a newly arrived brahmachari, "Are you reading any books these days, son?"

Br: "Yes, Amma. But most books say the same thing, and that is even repeated in many places in the same book."

Mother: "Son, there is only one thing to be said. What is everlasting, what is transitory? What is good, what is bad? How can one realize the eternal? The *Gita* and the *Puranas* (ancient scriptures) are all trying to explain these same things. The key principles are explained again and again. That is to show how important they are. They will stay in people's minds only if they hear them many times. There will be some apparent differences among the books, that is all: while the

Ramayana talks about the battle between Rama and Ravana, the *Mahabharata* talks about the war between the Kauravas and the Pandavas. The basic principle is the same. How should one hold on to it and move forward in the various situations that life brings? That is what all Mahatmas and all the books are trying to teach."

Another brahmachari: "Mother, my body feels very weak these days. It started after I took up yoga lessons."

Mother: "Son, when you start practicing yoga postures, you will feel fatigue for the first few months. You should eat well now. Once the body gets used to the practice, you will feel normal again. Then eating habits should also go back to normal!" (She laughs.) "Don't let me catch you stuffing yourself then, saying, 'Amma has told me to eat well...'"

Everybody laughs.

Mother continued, "Sadhaks should be very careful in their eating habits. It is better not to eat anything in the morning. You should immerse yourself in meditation until about eleven. The *tamasic* (dull) quality increases if you eat too much. The mind will have bad tendencies. If you do eat something in the morning, it should be very light. The mind should be concentrating on meditation."

A young man was sitting near the door of the meditation room, listening keenly to Amma's words. He came from Rishikesh, where he had lived for the last four years. He had a masters degree. He heard about Mother last month while visiting a friend in Delhi. He arrived at the Ashram two days ago to see Amma.

Young man: "Mother, I have been doing sadhana for the last few years. So far it has been disappointing. I lose my strength when I remember that I have not been able to realize God so far."

Mother: "Son, do you know what kind of detachment is needed for attaining God-realization? Imagine that you are sleeping soundly at home. Suddenly you wake up feeling very hot. You find that there is a fire raging all around you. Don't you get into a frenzy at that moment, trying to escape from the fire? There is that urgency with which you would cry for help then, seeing death in front of you have to cry with that same urgency to get the vision of God. Think how someone who falls into deep waters but can't swim, would struggle for breath - that is the struggle you should undergo to merge in the Supreme. You should constantly feel the grief of not having the vision of God. Your heart should constantly ache for it."

Mother stopped for a moment and continued, "Son, you won't get God's vision just by living in the ashram. You need to do sadhana with extreme detachment. You need to feel, 'I don't want anything but God.' To someone who has fever even sweet things will taste bitter. Similarly, if you have the fever of love for God, your mind will not go to anything else. Your eyes will not like to see anything but the form of God. Your ears will long to hear the Divine Name. All other sounds will irritate and burn your ears. Your mind will be struggling, like a fish out of water, till you reach God!" Mother closed Her eyes and remained immersed in meditation. Everyone sat watching Her intently. Amma got up after several minutes and walked along the outside wall of the meditation room. The tank for storing drinking water was just two feet away from the wall of the meditation room, on the south side, leaving a narrow passage in between. The water from this tank was pumped to another tank at a higher level from which it was distributed throughout.

Mother looked inside the tank before proceeding to the hut to give darshan to the devotees waiting there. She told the brahmacharis, "There is moss building up inside this tank, children. This should be cleaned soon!"

It is dusk. Mother is sitting on the cot in Her room singing a hymn, immersed in a divine mood. The flames in the oil lamps lit at dusk also remain still as if immersed in Her song.

Agamanta porule jaganmayi.

> *O essence of the Vedas, Who fills the universe,*
> *Who knows You Who are full of wisdom?*
> *O Blissful Self, Eternal Being devoid of sorrow,*
> *O Primal Power, Supreme Power, protect me!*
>
> *You are the dweller in all hearts, knowing all,*
> *Eager to offer the bliss of Liberation,*
> *Unseen by the wicked, but always shining*
> *in the meditation of the virtuous.*
>
> *O You shine forth in full*
> *In the form of Eternal truth,*
> *O Devi, Eternal One, show the Path of Salvation,*
> *and shine in me, a dullard among men.*
> *Clearly I tell You, O Mother*
> *Deign to enter and shine in my heart.*
> *Choose me to praise Your story*
> *And liberate me from this Maya.*

There was a picture of Devi Saraswati on the wall behind Amma. Did the Devi's fingers start playing the *vina* (stringed instrument) as Amma began singing? Even before the echo of Her song died down, Amma picked up the picture and kissed the Devi's image again and again. She held the picture against Her heart and sat still for a while.

She sat in the same pose without the slightest movement. As the evening bhajan started in the kalari, She gently put the picture down on the bed. Streams of tears were visible on the picture. She got up and began pacing back and forth slowly, immersed in Her divine mood.

The bhajan ended. The *arati* (vespers) also was over. Mother came down and started pacing in the small courtyard in front of the meditation room.

Advice to householders

The devotees who were standing at some distance now approached Mother. She brought them all to the kalari and sat down.

One devotee said, "Amma, I have a question on something you said to the brahmacharis this morning."

Mother: "What is it, son?"

Devotee: "Amma said that worldly life is equal to a dog's excreta. Should one view worldly life that badly?"

Amma (laughing): "Wasn't Amma talking to the brahmacharis then? They have to get that kind of detachment to persist on the spiritual path. A brahmachari who has a firm sense of his goal will not feel attracted to worldly life at all. Amma has to give him a low view of worldly life, so that he gets the strength to proceed to his goal. Otherwise, he will get trapped by physical pleasures and lose his strength.

"A soldier should get the training required for his work in the army and a policeman the training appropriate to his police duty. Similarly, the instructions needed for a brahmachari and a householder are different. Although the goal is the same for both, there is a difference in the level of intensity. The brahmachari has already renounced all his relations, and has dedicated himself totally to this path. He chants the mantra of detachment at every step.

"Mother would never say that *grihasthashrama* (married life) is inferior. Weren't all the ancient rishis householders? Didn't Rama and Krishna embrace the life of a householder? But someone who has taken the vow of *brahmacharya* (celibacy) has to view worldly life as equal to dog's excreta; only then will he be able to maintain the level of detachment needed to stay on the path.

"Thus a brahmachari should be given the advice needed for complete detachment. Amma is very happy to see the awakening of a sense of detachment in the householders among Her children. They only need to guard that flame from being extinguished; they can then reach the goal in time. Mother will not ask anyone to give up everything and become a *sannyasin* (renunciate) before he acquires a total sense of detachment.

"The path that Mother is prescribing is not one in which you go to the Himalayas and sit with your eyes closed thinking only of *moksha* (liberation). One has to learn to live according to the circumstances. The jackal thinks, as it sits in the jungle, that it won't howl the next time it sees a dog. But when it actually sees a dog, it cannot help howling out of sheer habit.

The man of real courage is one who has no attachment or sense of possession even when living in the midst of worldly experiences. The real *grihasthashrami* (married person) should be like that.

"Just as the flower falls away as the fruit takes shape, worldly desires will disappear when detachment ripens. No desire can bind such a person afterwards, whether he lives at home or in the forest. One who has set God-realization as his goal will not attach any importance to anything else. He has already understood that nothing physical is permanent and that real bliss is within."

Devotee: "How can we bring back the mind which goes in search of external pleasures?"

Mother: "The camel eats thorny bushes when it is hungry. Its mouth will start bleeding because of the thorns. Suppose you eat only hot peppers when you are hungry, because you like peppers. Your mouth will burn, and your stomach, too. You wanted to kill hunger, but now you have to bear pain. In the same way, if one depends on physical things for happiness, there will be sorrow in the end.

"Take the musk deer. However long it searches for the source of the fragrance of musk, it won't find it, because the fragrance comes from within itself. Bliss is not in external things; it is within oneself. Once you contemplate this and get enough detachment, the mind will not run after external pleasures.

"When we know the juice is inside the fruit, don't we peel the fruit and throw the peel away? That is the attitude a sadhak must have. Then the mind will not go outwards. He will be able to appreciate the essence of everything."

Devotee: "Isn't it possible to enjoy spiritual bliss while remaining in worldly life, Mother?"

Mother: "How can you experience spiritual bliss fully without fixing the mind totally in God? If you mix payasam with all the other dishes, can you enjoy its taste fully?

"Lord Vishnu (God, the Preserver) asked Sanaka (ancient sage) and the other sages several times to get married. But they replied, 'Every moment that we live in matrimony, will be spent without remembering you. We need only you, Lord! Nothing else.'

"Since nothing is separate from the Lord, worldly life is all right, some people argue. It is all right if one can remember God in every circumstance. But can we do that? What do we normally do when we eat something sweet - enjoy the sweet taste or remember the Lord? If you can think of nothing but the Lord even at that time, then there is no problem; you can go along that path."

Devotee: "Don't our scriptures prescribe four stages in life, namely, those of brahmacharya, grihasthashrama, *vanaprastha* (forest dweller) and *sannyasa* (state of renunciation)? After leading the life of a grihastha (householder), one goes into vanaprastha when one begins to have detachment. One becomes a sannyasin when one has complete detachment. All bonds are severed and one surrenders oneself completely to God. That is indeed the goal of life."

Another devotee: "It is also said that one can go from brahmacharya directly to sannyasa, if one has complete detachment."

Mother (laughing): "Sure, but parents don't allow it, that

is all. Some of the children at the Ashram had to overcome serious opposition to remain here."

Devotee: "Amma, do we deserve realization at all? We are so sorry that we are trapped in this worldly life!"

Mother: "Don't think like that, my dear children! Think that this is meant to remove all the obstacles on the path to God. If we see something hindering the path as we set out on a trip, we would remove it and then proceed. If not, it will always lie there as an obstacle. Worldly life allows us to uproot the desire and anger present in us. Amma sometimes recommends marriage for those children in whom the vasanas are very strong. If the vasanas are suppressed, they will explode sooner or later. We need to transcend them. Family life provides the circumstances for that. The mind should be given strength through contemplation. If a child falls down as it walks, it should get up and continue to walk. If it just lies there, it will never make progress. Family life is not meant to take us away from God. It is for bringing us closer to Him. Use it for that purpose, children, without worrying unnecessarily.

"Family life allows us to conquer our vasanas. Don't drown in the vasanas. Understand what they are and go beyond them. We will reach our goal only if we gain detachment in the face of vasanas. We feel satisfied after enjoying our fill of payasam. But a little later, we want twice as much. But when we understand the true nature of this yearning, the mind will not go after it. Would anyone touch the payasam if a lizard falls into it? When the vasanas pull us towards them, the mind would resist if it knows that they are not the source of real happiness and that they will only bring us sorrow later. But this knowledge has to be firmly planted in the mind and intellect. Don't let your lives go to waste, children, by being slaves to your minds! Don't barter away a priceless jewel for a piece of candy. Our minds will become more quiet if we stop giving as much importance to sensory pleasures as we do now. Don't worry if you don't get the strength to do so right away! Sit in solitude for a little while every day, and reflect on this, assuming the attitude of a witness. Make it a regular habit. You will certainly discover the required strength. No use sitting somewhere and crying that you are weak. Find the strength needed. Then you will be able to stand up to any challenge, without faltering. Don't shed tears thinking that you are undeserving, children! That will only rob your strength.

"Son, don't regret that you couldn't become a brahmachari or that you can't be near Amma all the time. You children are all like the leaves on a plant. Some leaves are close to the flower and others far from it, but all the leaves are on the same plant. Likewise all are Amma's children; don't doubt that at all. Don't feel sorry that you can't enjoy Mother's presence by being near Her. You can also reach there one day."

Devotee: "Still, haven't our lives been wasted by being trapped in all these worldly desires?"

Mother: "Son, why should you feel sorry about the past? Go forward with faith.

"Once there was a woodcutter. He was very poor. He would go to the forest daily, cut wood, make charcoal from it and bring it to a store that sold it as fuel. He had only a very small income from this, not at all enough to fill his belly. He had just a rotting, leaky old, hut for a house. His health did not allow him to work any harder. He was always in despair. One day the king passed through the village. He heard about the sad plight of the poor woodcutter. The king told him, 'You don't have to struggle from now on. I am giving you a sandalwood forest. You can live comfortably with the income from it.'

"The next day, the woodcutter went to work as usual. Since he had his own forest, he did not have to search for trees to cut. He cut some sandalwood, made charcoal and brought it to the fuel store as usual. He didn't earn any more from it than he usually did.

"After a few years, the king came to the village again. He asked for the man to whom he had given the sandalwood forest. The king expected him to be a rich man by now. He was astonished when he saw the woodcutter. If anything, the man was poorer than before. There was no happiness on his face at all. He had even forgotten how to laugh. The king asked him in dismay, 'What happened to you? What did you do with the forest I gave you?' 'I cut the trees and sold them as charcoal,' the man said. The king couldn't believe that he had given away those precious trees for some paltry sums of money. 'Are there any trees left,' he asked. 'Yes, there is one,' said the man. The king replied, 'Oh, you fool! What I had given you was a forest full of sandalwood trees. They were not meant to be burnt as fuel! All right, at least there is one tree left. Cut it and sell it without turning it into charcoal. You will get enough for the rest of your life from it.' The woodcutter followed the king's advice and was able to live comfortably thereafter.

"Children, you have the desire to know God. That is enough. Your lives will be fulfilled. It is enough if you lead a proper life in the future."

A woman came with two little children and prostrated.

CHAPTER 1

She put her head on Mother's lap and started to cry bitterly. She told the story of her grief.

Her husband had started a business with money borrowed at an exorbitant rate of interest. The business failed. They sold their land and pawned the woman's jewelry to pay back the debt. They could not reclaim the jewelry in time, so it was auctioned off. Due to the pressure from creditors, they sold their house and rented a place. Now there is no money to pay the rent. The woman set out with her children with the idea of committing suicide. At that point, she heard about Amma from a friend and has come to see Her.

She said through her tears, "Amma, do you know what a comfortable life we had? My husband has ruined everything. I cannot live there any longer. There is no money for even the rent. All my relatives are doing well. How can I show my face to them? I decided to end this life along with my children."

Mother: "Daughter, you don't have to die because of this. Is death in our hands, anyway? And, what right do you have to take the lives of your children?

"Where there is fire, there is also smoke, my child. If there is desire, there is also sorrow. Like the sun and its heat. You wanted a grand life, so you started a big business. That has caused grief. If you had learnt to be satisfied with what you had, there wouldn't be any problem now. Life is full of happiness and sorrow. There is no life which is all happiness or all sorrow.

"There is a time for everything. At certain times in our lives, everything we start ends in failure. No use collapsing when that happens. Hold on tightly to the Lord. He is our sole refuge. He will not fail to show a way out. At least you have your health; you can work for a living. The Lord will arrange that. No need to sit in a corner and cry; that will just waste time and ruin your health as well. Don't grieve over what is gone, my daughter! Remembering what is past and mourning is like cuddling a corpse.

"The past will never come back to us, daughter! We don't know about the future, either. Instead of wasting your time and ruining your health thinking about them, what you should do is to strengthen the present. You are now ruining the present by dwelling constantly on the past and the future. Only the Paramatman knows about all three - past, present and future. Therefore, you should surrender all three to Him and go forward, always remembering Him. Then there will be a smile on your face, always.

"Picture someone eating ice cream. As he eats, he thinks, 'In the restaurant I went to yesterday, all the food was exposed. Could some cockroach or lizard have fallen in? Was my headache this morning caused by eating that food? Oh, this morning, my son asked for new clothes again. How can I buy anything for him? Where is the money? For how long have I been dreaming about a better house! What I make is not enough for anything. Things will get better only if I find a better job.' All the ice cream is gone by this time. Immersed in his thoughts, the man didn't even know its taste. The past was disturbing his mind, the future was also causing worry and he wasted a pleasant occasion in the present. If, instead, he had forgotten about the past and the future and paid attention to the present moment, he could have enjoyed the flavor of the ice cream at least. Therefore, taste every moment as you go forward, children! Surrender everything to Him, or greet all circumstances with a smile. Forget the past and the future, and deal with the matters at hand now, with alertness.

"If you fall, get up and go forward with enthusiasm. Consider that the fall was meant to make you more alert. See the past as a canceled check. There is no point in brooding over it. It is useless just to sit and worry about your wounds; you have to apply medicine promptly.

"Daughter, no one brings anything to this world or takes anything away. We get things here and then we lose them. That is all. Once we recognize that this is the nature of things, we will not lose our strength worrying about them. Real wealth is peace of mind, daughter! We should find a way to guard that.

"Stay here until your husband gets a job. Your children can stay here, too. Stop worrying!"

With Her hands, Amma wiped away the woman's tears, and all her worries.

Another woman said, "Amma, I am very sad when I feel unable to connect my mind with God. And many bad thoughts come up and trouble me."

Amma: "Daughter, don't fret about bad thoughts. The mind is just a collection of thoughts. Think that the bad thoughts come up because it is time for them to disappear. But be careful not to identify with them.

"When we travel in a bus, we see so many nice things on the way - nice houses, pretty flowers, beautiful gardens. But we don't form any bonds with them, we just pass by, because, they are not our real goal. We have to learn to see the thoughts passing through our minds in the same way. Watch them, but don't relate to them. Don't cling to them. We can stand on the bank and watch a river flow. It is interesting. But if we jump in, we will soon lose our strength. Try to develop the ability to stay back as a witness while thoughts pass through your mind, daughter. That will add strength to your mind."

A woman who had been listening to Mother's words from the beginning, said: "Amma, once we are entangled in the web of family life, it is difficult to break loose, however much we try!"

Mother: "Daughter, a bird sits on a dry twig on a tree and eats the fruit it found somewhere. It knows that the twig may break at any moment. So it is very alert while sitting. You should see that this world also has only that much reality. Everything may be lost, at any moment. You should remember that, children. Be sure to hold on to the truth that God is the only lasting thing. Then there will be no reason for sorrow.

"If we are aware that there are fireworks going on around us, the next loud bang won't startle us and make us lose our balance. In the same way, if we understand the true nature of this world, we won't lose our equilibrium. We should learn to do everything as a duty assigned to us, and go on without identifying with anything. Look at a bank manager. Look at all the people who work under him. He has to pay attention to them. And he has to deal with all the loan applicants. They bring a lot of supporting documents. If the manager is charmed by the smiles and complimentary words of the applicants and gives them all loans without inspecting their documents carefully, he will end up in jail tomorrow. He knows that some of these people have come to get money from him by whatever means. He knows that the money in the bank is not his own, yet he just doesn't give it away to anyone who asks. He doesn't show annoyance to anyone and doesn't hesitate to give loans to those who deserve them. He just does his duty properly, that is all, so he will not have any reason to be sorry. We should all be like that. We should be able to do everything with sincerity and enthusiasm. We should not be discouraged or become lazy, thinking that nothing is going to be with us in the end. We should do our work as a duty, with shraddha. There should be no hatred towards it. See everything as a face of the Paramatman. Everything is that same ultimate principle.

"Haven't you seen candies wrapped in paper of different colors - red and white, blue and green? All different outside. Kids will fight for their favorite colors, 'I want blue,' 'I want red,' and so on. The one who wants red will not be happy if we give him blue. He will cry till he gets the red ones. But when the wrappers are removed, all the candies taste the same. We are like these kids now. We don't think about the candy; we are fascinated by the wrappers and fight over them. In reality, the principle that dwells in all living things is the same. Even though the outer color or shape may differ, the supreme principle does not change. We are now unable to grasp this because we have lost our child-like innocence and our inner purity.

"Let us say someone is angry with us or acts in a hostile manner. If we react to him in anger or punish him, it is like poking a wound he has on his hand, and making it larger, instead of putting some medicine on it and healing it. The pus from his wound will fall on our body, and make us also stink. His ego becomes stronger, while our ignorance deepens. On the other hand, if we forgive him, it is like applying medicine on his wounds. That enlarges our minds. Therefore, lead a life of love and forgiveness, children. All this may seem very difficult. But if you try, you will certainly succeed."

Devotee: "Amma, where can we find time for meditation and japa in the midst of all the responsibilities of family life?"

Mother: "Nothing is difficult for those who really want it. You have to have a sincere desire to do it. You should spend at least one day a week in solitude, performing sadhana. You may have responsibilities and jobs to do. Even then, one day should be set apart. Don't you take sick leave if you are not well, even if there is a lot of unfinished work? Don't you take a day off to attend the wedding of a relative? How much more important is this! So, at least one day a week, go to an ashram and do sadhana and *seva* (service). That day will be a training for strengthening love and cooperation in the family as well.

"When your children indulge in mischief, explain things to them with love. Childhood is the foundation for life. If we don't pay attention to them and show them love, they may go astray. Parents should remember specially to give them love in their tender age, just as you would water a tender young plant. Once the children are grown and have found jobs, the parents should entrust family responsibilities to them, and retire to an ashram life and do sadhana in solitude. Purify the mind through service. It is not wise to cling to your home and children till the last breath. When the children are grown up, then the desire to see grandchildren and to help with their upbringing will become strong! All the living beings on earth manage to grow and survive, don't they? They are not waiting for help, are they? Leave your children in God's hands. That is what loving parents should do. That is indeed true love.

"Until now, we have toiled for 'my sake and for my children.' There is no difference in this between us and the animals. Then, what is the fruit of this precious human life of ours?

From now on, our work should be for 'your sake.' Then, the 'I' will slowly disappear by itself. Our worries and sorrows will disappear, as well.

"Once we board a train, why continue to carry our load and complain how heavy it is? We can put it down. Similarly, learn to take refuge in the Supreme, and surrender everything totally, children!

"If once a week is not practical, at least two days a month should be spent in an ashram atmosphere, immersed in japa and meditation and doing service. Remembering God is the real foundation for life. In due course one can free oneself from all bonds, just as a snake sheds its skin, and merge in Him. Follow a regular discipline. Some people say the world around is also Brahman, so why withdraw from it? Yes, everything is Brahman, but have we reached that stage? God cannot see wrongs in anyone. He sees only the good in everything. When we get that same attitude, then there is some meaning in saying 'everything is Brahman.' If there is one thing right among even a thousand wrongs, God will see only that.

"A guru had two disciples. He used to give one of them more responsibilities in the ashram. The second disciple did not like this, since he considered himself to be the best in the ashram. He began to dislike the first disciple. One day he asked the guru, 'Why are you not entrusting me with any of the ashram matters? I can do these things better than he can.'

"The guru called both disciples and asked them to go out and learn about the nature of people. As the first disciple walked along, he saw a man giving candy and consoling a small child on the roadside. Upon inquiry, he came to know that the man was, in fact, a murderer. Still, the disciple was pleased at the good side of the man. As he walked on, he saw someone giving water to an old man who was lying on the wayside, weakened by hunger and thirst. The disciple came to know that the person who was doing this was a robber. He was glad that there was compassion even in the robber. Next he saw a woman wiping the tears of another woman and soothing her. The kind woman was a prostitute. The disciple could not look down on the prostitute as he saw the compassion in her heart. He came back to the guru and described everything, giving special praise for the good actions he saw.

"The second disciple also came back by this time. He reported that he saw a man beating a child. Next he saw someone rebuking a beggar. Further along, he saw a nurse being very cross with a patient. These sights only generated hatred in the heart of the disciple towards the people he saw. The man who was beating the child had a big heart; in fact, he fed and clothed many poor children and paid for their education. This one child had the habit of stealing things. Talking to him did not help and the man finally resorted to beating him, to make him see his mistake. But the disciple could not justify this. Should anyone, however good-hearted, be allowed to beat a child? Bad fellow! The second man he had encountered was one who gave generously to others. He saw a healthy man begging and was trying to persuade him to use his God-given health and work for a living. The disciple didn't approve of even this. However generous one might be, what right does he have to berate someone? If he didn't want to give anything, he could just send the beggar away. Lastly, the nurse the disciple saw was one who loved her patients very much. She nursed patients day and night. This particular patient had the habit of removing his bandages. This delayed the healing of his wounds. The nurse was scolding him for this, out of love for him. Well, the disciple didn't like this either. The nurse must have applied some medicine that caused burning; that is probably why the patient removed the bandages. And she is scolding him for that, wicked woman!

"The guru listened to the explanations given by both of his disciples. Then he said, 'No one is totally bad in this world. However bad someone is said to be, there will be something good in him. One of you could see the good in a murderer, a robber and a prostitute. If there is goodness in us, we can see it in others also. We need the kind of eyes which do that.'

"The guru then said to the second disciple, 'My son, you saw your own nature in others also. You could see only bad things even in those who had much goodness in them. The day this nature of yours changes, you will be able to see goodness in everything.'

"Now our mind is like the second disciple's. Even if there are a thousand rights, we don't see them; we see the one wrong that may be there. But the Lord sees only whatever is good in His children. Only when we have this attitude, can we say all is Brahman or all is God.

"There are people who ask, 'Isn't the guru within us? Isn't it enough to follow our own minds? Why should we take refuge in someone else?' Sure, the guru is within us; but it is a guru who is the slave of our vasanas now. Our minds are not under our control, they are under the control of the vasanas. Therefore, it is dangerous to follow our minds. Mother will tell you the story of a man who approached many gurus. All of them talked only about humility, faith and devotion. The man didn't like this. 'I don't like to be anybody's slave,' he decided. He sat on the side of the road, and said to himself, 'The gurus I saw are not fit to guide me properly.' As he looked ahead thinking this, he saw a camel, which was grazing nearby, nodding its head. The man was surprised that the camel understood what he was thinking. This must be the guru I have been searching for. He approached the camel and asked. 'Will you be my guru?' The camel nodded its ahead again. The man was happy.

"After this, the man did nothing without first asking the camel guru. The camel agreed to everything he asked, by nodding its head. One day he asked the camel, 'I have seen a girl. May I love her?' The camel nodded. After a few days, he came to the camel again, and asked, 'Shall I marry her?' The camel guru gave its approval to this, too.

A few more days passed. The next question was, 'Is it all right if one drinks a little?' The camel nodded again. The man came home very drunk that day. Soon this became a habit. His wife did not approve. He came to the guru and asked if it was all right if he fought with his wife. Again, the guru agreed. Soon the man came back to ask, 'My wife does not like my drinking. Shall I kill her?' The camel nodded its head even on this occasion. The man hurried home and stabbed his wife, injuring her seriously. The police came and arrested him. He was given a life imprisonment.

"Our mind is like this camel guru. There is no question of right or wrong. It approves of everything that pleases us. There is no thought of future consequences. If we depend on such a mind, which is a slave of vasanas, we will get only eternal bondage. Our intellect does not have discrimination now. The best course is to follow the advice of a real guru. Today we do wrong things, under the excuse that God is making us do them. It is not right to insist that the guru should do what we tell him. Only one who follows the guru's instructions without questioning will be able to reach the goal. He is the true disciple.

" Just a thought from the guru is enough to take the disciple to his goal - just as the tortoise can hatch its eggs by thinking about it. A Satguru is one who has realized the Truth. Following his advice will take us higher, even if it seems inconvenient to follow right now. Those who agree to all the wishes of the disciples are not real gurus. They know only how to nod their heads, like the camel. They don't think of the progress of the disciples."

A devotee: "Don't the scriptures say 'All is Brahman,' Amma?"

Mother: "But we have not reached that stage! Therefore, we have to act with discrimination. It is not wise to go near a rabid dog, declaring everything is Brahman. The friend who asks you to stay away from the dog is also Brahman! If you don't have the discrimination to decide on the right course of action in this case, your life will be ruined, indeed.

"As long as we have not experienced it, what is the use of saying 'all is Brahman?' Take, for instance, items made of cane. There is cane in the chair, in the table and in the basket. Also, we have to see that the cane contains within it the chair, the table and the basket. Similarly, there is gold in the ring, the bracelet, and the earrings. But we are mostly enamored by the external shapes of these things. Those who are not fascinated by the form, see the gold that is in all of them. We have to develop that kind of vision. We have to grasp that everything contains the one ultimate truth - Brahman. Those who are at that stage cannot do anything wrong. Those who just have 'Brahman' on their lips, but have not experienced it, are the ones who commit mistakes.

"*Advaita* (nonduality) is the state where there is no more than one. It is the state in which you spontaneously see everyone else as identical to you. It is not something you talk about, it is a state of being.

"Once a man borrowed money from several people and bought an island. There he built a palace for himself. When anybody visited him, he talked only about his palace and about his own importance. One day a sannyasin came there for *bhiksha* (alms). The rich man felt that the sannyasin did not show enough respect to him and was annoyed. He told the sannyasin, 'Do you know who owns this island, this palace and everything here? All these belong to me. I control everything. No one has shown disrespect to me so far!'

"The sannyasin listened to everything, and then asked, 'Does everything here belong to you?'

'Yes,' came the reply.

'Truly?'

'Yes, truly.'

"The sannyasin said, 'Whose money bought all these things? Ask your conscience that question!'

"The rich man was abashed by this. He realized his mistake. There was nothing there that belonged to him. He fell at the feet of the *sadhu* (monk).

"The 'knowledge' we have now is not something gained through sadhana. We have just read what others have written, and we sit around mouthing the words, 'I am Brahman.' We say 'I am Brahman,' but we do not show any compassion or humility or forgiveness to anyone. Such people have no right even to utter the word 'Brahman.' If you train a parrot, it will also say 'Brahman, Brahman.' But if a cat comes by, the parrot will only know how to cry in fear. It will die crying. Instead of just repeating the word 'Brahman,' we have to absorb that principle. We have to fix it in our minds through constant contemplation. That principle is the symbol of compassion and broadmindedness. It has to be experienced. Those who have experienced it don't have to keep saying, 'I am Brahman.' We can feel it just by going near them. Their smile will persist in all circumstances. Now the Brahman in us is like the tree in a seed. How will it sound if the seed claims, 'I am the tree?' The tree is in the seed. But the seed has to go under the soil, then the sprout and the seedling has to grow up. When it becomes a tree, you can chain even an elephant to it. But if we don't protect the seed, it will be eaten by some bird. The Supreme Principle is indeed within us, but we have to bring it to the plane of experience through study and constant meditation.

"Once, a young man approached a guru and requested to be taken as a disciple. It was an ashram with many aspirants. The guru told the youth, 'Spiritual life is very hard. It is better if you go now and come back at a later time.'

"The young man was very disappointed. Seeing this, the guru asked, 'All right, what work can you do?' He named several jobs, but the young man was not used to any of those. 'Then, can you look after our horses?'

"The young man said, 'As you wish.'

"He was put in charge of the horses. The new disciple

did his duty with great dedication. Soon the horses became healthier and stronger.

"The guru usually did not give any special instructions to his disciples. Every morning, he would give them a verse which they had to contemplate and put to practice in their lives. That was the method of teaching he followed.

"One morning, the guru began earlier than usual. He gave the disciples their daily verses and was about to depart on a journey on one of the horses, when the young disciple came running for his instruction. He was busy with his work and could not come when the guru called earlier. 'O master,' he asked, 'what is my lesson for today?' The guru replied sternly, 'Don't you know I am going on a journey? Is this the time for this question?' He then mounted his horse and trotted off. The youth was not disappointed. He started meditating on the guru's words, 'Don't you know I am going on a journey? Is this the time for this question?'

"The guru returned in the evening. He couldn't find the young man among the other disciples. The guru asked about him. The others said in ridicule, 'That silly fellow is sitting somewhere muttering something like, 'Don't you know I am going on a journey? Is this the time for this question?"' All of them started laughing. The guru understood what happened. He called the young man and asked what he was doing. He said, 'Master, I was contemplating what you said to me this morning.' The guru's eyes filled with tears. He put his hands on the disciple's head and blessed him. The other aspirants did not like this at all. They let the guru know their complaint: 'Master, you ignored all of us who have been here for so long. Why give so much love to that fool?'

"The guru asked one of them to go and get some intoxicating substance. When the intoxicant came, he mixed it in water and poured a little into everyone's mouth and asked them to spit it out immediately. Then, he asked, 'Did anyone feel any intoxication?'

'How is that possible? Didn't you ask us to spit it out right away?'

"The guru said, 'It is the same way in which you took my morning instructions also. You heard it and forgot it immediately. But the young man you are complaining about is not like that. He accepted whatever I told him, without seeing even a trace of negativity in it. He has that innocence in him. Besides, when the horses were in your charge, they were just skin and bones, because you didn't feed them properly. You didn't wash them. They were irritable and would kick anyone who approached them. But when I put him in charge, the horses became healthy and gained weight. Now if anyone approaches them, they will come closer and show love by the movement of their heads. He gave them not only food, but love as well. He did his duty sincerely and regularly. He did each action as his duty, for its own sake. Above all, he was able to absorb my words totally, without questioning.'

"Children, we have to be like that. We shouldn't see any word of the guru as meaningless. We should be ready to reflect on his words and assimilate them totally. The guru cannot withhold his grace from flowing to anyone who does that."

One woman among the devotees asked, "Amma, if someone gets detachment after he is married, is it proper for him to forsake his wife and children?" Her husband was standing next to her. He laughed when he heard his wife's question. Everybody else joined in the laughter.

Mother (laughing): "Don't be afraid, my daughter. *Mon* (son) will not leave you and come here. If he does, we will make him run back to you." Everyone laughs.

Mother continued, "Once you are married, you cannot abandon everything just like that and leave. But if you have achieved intense detachment, and if there is enough wealth for the family to live without you, then you can renounce everything. But the detachment has to be real, like the detachment Buddha and Ramatirtha had.

"It is never right to enter sannyasa just to escape from one's responsibilities. The sense of detachment has to be ripe. Otherwise, it would be like prematurely breaking open an egg that is being hatched."

A devotee: "Amma, I don't feel like going to work at all now. There is no value for truth or dharma there. My coworkers harm me in many ways if I don't dance to their tune."

Mother: "This problem is not just yours, son, many of the children who come here complain about this. These days, it is difficult to do your work honestly. Truth and dharma have no value. We are suffering the consequences of that. Those who go out into the world to work will have to overcome many obstacles. Those who stick to truth and honesty may be troubled by the deeds of their colleagues. But what is the use of being sorry and weak? Son, don't pay attention to what others are doing. Act according to your own conscience. God will not abandon those who do that. Those who do wrong, just for immediate gains, are not aware of the suffering that lies ahead.

They will have to undergo the punishment for their actions, tomorrow if not today."

Mother stopped briefly, and then asked, "What time is it, children?"

A devotee: "It is past eleven."

Mother: "You go to bed now, children. Mother hasn't yet read the letters that came this morning. Let Mother go to Her room."

She got up. As She neared the steps leading up to Her room, a devotee came running and prostrated.

Mother: "What is it, son?"

Devotee: 'I am leaving early in the morning, Amma. I won't be able to see you before I leave. That is why I am troubling you now."

Mother (laughing): "How can it be a trouble for Amma?"

Devotee: "I didn't get a chance to tell you the reason for my visit, Amma. My daughter's wedding is next week. Everything has worked out as you said. I don't have to give even a *paisa* (Indian coin) as dowry. The boy is working in the Persian Gulf area. He says he will be taking her there. His family is pretty well off financially."

This man had been trying to arrange his daughter's marriage for seven years. Planet Mars was not favorable in her horoscope. They considered many marriage proposals. Most of the time, the horoscopes didn't match; even when they matched, somehow the proposals fell through. The father was feeling anxious about this whole matter when he heard about Mother three months ago. He came with his daughter to see Amma. Mother gave a mantra to the daughter and said, "There is no need to run around for this anymore. You chant this mantra with devotion, daughter, and everything will be all right." Three weeks later, a marriage proposal was brought in by a distant relative of theirs. The horoscopes matched very well and a date was fixed for the wedding quickly.

"I have here the wedding ring for the boy. Amma, please bless it!" He gave a small packet to Mother. She held it to Her eyes and gave it back.

Mother went to Her room. Leelabai, a householder devotee, was waiting outside the door of Mother's room. She was unhappy that her *tali*[3] was lost somewhere.

Mother said, "Didn't you bring it to give to Amma, daughter! Think that God has taken it. Why feel sorry about it?"

Leela was from Kottayam. Her younger daughter lived at the Ashram and went to school from there. Leela's father didn't like his granddaughter living at the Ashram.

Mother: "How is your father?"

Leela: "He doesn't like our coming here at all. He scolds us for it all the time."

Mother: "But that is normal! Who likes to see the daughters of the family going on the spiritual path?"

Leela: "Amma, aren't you the one who causes all this disapproval?"

Mother: "Oh, really? Who says that?" (She laughs.)

"When you enter a spiritual life, you are likely to hear many objections. Only when you overcome them and move beyond, it becomes clear how strong your bond to God is. If your father is angry with you, it is his samskara. Why worry about it? Coming to the Ashram is your samskara.

---

[3] A small pendant traditionally worn by married women.

"Suppose strong winds and heavy rain start just as we are about to go somewhere. If we become scared and stay inside, we will not, of course, reach our destination. One who has a sincere desire to reach the goal has to ignore these obstacles and go forward. If you just remain indoors, it shows that you don't yearn for the goal that much.

"Strive to reach the goal, transcending whatever the obstacles may be - that is real courage. Others will voice their opinion, each according to his background. Give them only the importance they deserve. But do not hate them. There is no need to fret about what they said."

Mother went into Her room.

The midnight moon peered into the room through the window curtains. Amma is writing letters to Her children all over the world, many of them fast asleep at this hour. She is wiping their tears with Her words.

When She saw that the brahmacharini, who had been taking dictation, had fallen asleep over the sheets of paper, Amma took the pen in Her hand. She started applying the cool sandal paste of Her consoling words to the burning minds of Her children everywhere. Perhaps, She was entering their dreams at this time, causing their dry, parched lips to slowly light up with a smile.

CHAPTER TWO

Wednesday, June 26, 1985

Devotion

Mother and the brahmacharis are in the meditation room. There are also some householder devotees like Padmanabhan and Divakaran.

Padmanabhan is from Kozhikode. He is a bank official. He mentioned the recent visit of a homeopathic doctor and family to the Ashram.

Mother: "Amma remembers them. He considers himself to be a great believer in Advaita. But his wife is full of devotion. Perhaps he came for darshan because she asked him to. He put on big airs as he came in. There is no Rama or Krishna, he said. Amma said, 'Everyone ultimately reaches the same place. But you need an *upadhi* (an instrument or prop) for sadhana. And, how can you say there is no Rama or Krishna? Even if you don't see Ochira[4] on a map of India, can you say there is no place called Ochira? Our sense of advaita is just limited to our words. It is not possible to bring it into our experience without devotion.' He did not say anything after that."

Mother took up a pen lying nearby and wrote 'Namah Shivaya' on Her left forearm and sat looking at it. It seemed

---
[4] A place near Mother's Ashram.

that as She wrote that name, She entered into a divine mood.

Mother said to Padmanabhan who was looking intently at the mantra written on Her forearm, "In the early days, Amma used to hold the pillow close to Her heart when She went to bed. She would kiss the pillow repeatedly. She could not see it as a pillow; She felt it was Devi. Sometimes She would lie there with Her lips to the wall, imagining She was kissing the Divine Mother, or She would write 'Namah Shivaya' on the pillow and mat and kiss the Name. She wouldn't fall asleep before She nearly fell unconscious, calling Devi again and again, crying to Her."

Mother became silent and sat still. Her eyes closed slowly. One could see on Her face the waves of bliss that were rising inside Her. Everyone sat in meditation, with eyes riveted on Amma.

A brahmachari sang the song, *'Mouna ghanamrita santiniketam.'*

> *In the abode of impenetrable Silence*
> *Of eternal beauty and peace*
> *Where the mind of Gautama Buddha was dissolved*
> *In the Effulgence that destroys all bonds*
> *On the Shore of Bliss*
> *Which lies beyond the reach of thought...*
>
> *In the knowledge that bestows eternal harmony*
> *The Abode without beginning or end*
> *The Bliss known only when*
> *The movements of the mind subside*
> *At the Seat of Power*
> *The Region of utter Consciousness...*

> *At the Goal that bestows the sweet State*
> *of eternal non-duality*
> *Described as 'Thou art That'*
> *That is the place where I long to reach*
> *But I can only do so through Your Grace.*

The song ended. Mother opened Her eyes after a little while.

The nature of the Guru

Divakaran: "I have a friend. He lived with a *swami* (ordained monk) for some time and received a mantra from him. One day the swami scolded him for something. My friend left that day."

Mother: "Son, in spiritual life, if you accept someone as your guru, you should have complete faith and dedication towards him. Sometimes, the guru may be very stern, for the good of the disciples. But the disciple should never find fault with the guru. Gurus show sternness without identifying with it. A mother may beat a child to stop it from putting its hand in the fire. Is she doing it out of some spite towards the child? No, it is only to save the child from danger. Your friend should have understood that it was for his own good that the guru had scolded him."

Divakaran: "He said that he left because he could not emulate many of the things the guru did."

Mother: "Disciples should not do everything the guru does. That will hinder their progress. No one can emulate the guru completely. We should decide, through discrimination, those actions of the guru which will be beneficial to us, and copy only such actions. One should never think, 'Didn't my guru do this, so why can't I do the same thing?' The Mahatmas who have attained completeness have no bonds. They are like the giant trees to which even elephants can be chained. There is no need of a fence around such trees. But we are like small plants. We have to fear the cows and the goats. We need a fence to protect ourselves from them. The actions of Mahatmas are not like ours. We should not copy all their actions.

"Actions of a normal human being arise from the belief, 'I am this body.' But a Mahatma lives with the understanding that he is pure consciousness. Therefore, many of his actions will be difficult for ordinary people to understand.

"Once there was a Mahatma. Every morning, he would boil some oil and immediately pour it on his body. Then he would proceed to take his bath. One of the disciples who saw this, thought that this must be the source of all the powers the guru had. The next day, he also boiled some oil and poured it on himself. You can guess the consequences! (Everyone laughs.) If we imitate everything the guru does, this may become our experience also. Therefore, we should adopt only those things that would benefit each of us."

Sadhana is indispensable

Divakaran: "I have not seen in any of the other ashrams I have visited, a routine similar to what is followed here. I see that meditation and *karma yoga* (action dedicated to God) are stressed here. In many other places, scriptural study is given the highest importance."

Mother: "As long as thoughts about worldly affairs bother

us, we need to practice a strict routine of japa and meditation to rise above them. It is necessary to put a lot of effort into this practice in the beginning. In due course, it will become natural. Only through sadhana one makes progress. Without sadhana, you have nothing. What is the use of studying books and giving speeches? What difference is there between one who gives speeches and a tape recorder? He will just mouth what he has learned, that is all. Will our hunger be satisfied by reading cookbooks? We have to cook something and eat. *Tapas* (austerity) is what is needed. It will enhance the good qualities and good vasanas in us. The purity and concentration of mind are most important.

"Amma is not saying that one need not study the scriptures. Along with study, sadhana is needed. Sadhana is the primary thing. There should not be a lapse in it. Sadhana should become our nature just like brushing our teeth and bathing.

"When we come out into the world after being trained in the Ashram, dressed in the clothes given by the Ashram, thousands of people will love and respect us. But Amma says to Her children that those who call them bad names are their greatest gurus. Only such unpleasant treatment will make us look at ourselves carefully. When there are only people who love us, we won't examine ourselves. When others show hostility, we should enquire, 'Why are they hostile to me? What mistake have I made to deserve such treatment?' Thus, the accusations against us will become steps leading to our growth."

Padmanabhan: "Mother, what is best - trying for our own liberation first or working for the good of others?"

Mother: "The selfishness in us has to go completely before we can think solely of the good of others, doesn't it? We should strive to achieve such a state of mind first. Our prayers and our actions to achieve that state of mind form the path to liberation. We need to forget ourselves completely and to think only of the welfare of others. When we dedicate ourselves solely to the well being of others, it is our own mind that becomes pure."

A brahmachari, who was listening to this conversation, asked about the power of the guru. Amma said in reply, "There are different kinds of gurus. Satgurus can bestow liberation merely by their *sankalpa* (resolve). Even their breath is beneficial to nature."

Br: "It is said the guru will protect the disciples from all dangers. If a danger comes to a disciple when the guru is in *samadhi* (absorption), how will he know about it and give protection?"

Mother: "After all, no one is separate from the Self. Isn't everyone contained in the Self? Even though a river has two separate banks, there is only one river bed. When the guru is in samadhi, he is merged in the Self. He will know about the situation."

The greatness of devotion

Padmanabhan: "Amma, a lot of people don't recognize the greatness of devotion at all. Many of the people who go to temples and pray daily don't seem to lead very spiritual lives."

Mother: "There is a belief that devotion means going to a lot of temples to worship a hundred different deities. The devotion of such people is a blind faith which is not based on an understanding of the principles. Others who see this, think that devotion means only this, and they speak ill of devotion.

Spiritual people will not oppose *tattvattile bhakti* ('devotion in principle'). We should understand that God realization is the aim of life and worship Him with this goal firmly fixed in our mind. 'Devotion in principle' means recognizing that it is one and the same Lord who manifests in all living beings and in all the deities, under all names and forms, and surrendering selflessly to Him. That is the kind of devotion we should have.

"It is hard to become established in *jnana* (spiritual wisdom), without devotion. With gravel alone we cannot build anything; we need to add cement also and make concrete. We cannot build the steps leading to God without adding the cement of love.

"There may be many types of dishes, but those who have indigestion or other illnesses cannot eat everything. But *kanji* (gruel) made with broken rice is agreeable to everyone's health. The path of devotion is like that. It suits everyone.

"When the sense of 'I' persists, we need a center (*upadhi*) to focus our minds on so that we can eliminate the ego. Devotion is the love for that center. It is the intense eagerness to realize the goal. Devotion is like the tincture used for cleaning a wound; it cleans the mind.

"The field that is the mind should be irrigated with the water of devotion, and then the seed of knowledge can be sown. Then we can harvest the crop of liberation. Anyone who has tasted *premabhakti* - devotion that is pure, deep love - even for a second, will never waver from it. But such devotion is not born in everyone. Not everyone who enters the lottery gets the first prize. That goes only to one person among millions. True loving devotion is like that, only one in a million gets it."

In the middle of this praise of the greatness of devotion,

Mother became silent. Her mind left the external world and soared to some higher plane. She sat still, with eyes half-closed. Her motionless form reminded everyone of the Divine Mother who is beyond all attributes, and who does everything while appearing to be actionless.

The duality embraced for the sake of devotion is more beautiful, indeed, than nonduality!

Mother opened Her eyes a little later. But She was not in a mood to talk. Her face showed that She was in some other world. Was this the same Mother who was so eloquent, just a few minutes ago?

A few more minutes passed. Mother went near a child and gave him two chocolates from the packet a devotee had offered Her. Planting a kiss on the head of the child, Mother said: "This chocolate gives sweetness now, but it will harm your teeth later. If you know God, you can enjoy sweetness all the time. It is not bad for the teeth either!"

From the meditation room, Mother went to the darshan hut. All the devotees who were waiting there came near Her one by one and prostrated. One woman embraced Mother tightly and started crying. She had been married for many years, but had no children. That was the cause of her grief.

Mother: "Daughter, you are crying because you have no children. Those who have children shed tears when they see the behavior of their children!"

Mother pulled the woman up and wiped her tears with Her hand, saying, "Don't worry, daughter. You pray to God. Amma will make a sankalpa for you."

Rays of expectation and hope shone on the woman's face.

Mother's instructions

Mother asked a child sitting nearby to sing a *kirtan* (devotional song). The sweet sound gently flowed, without a trace of bashfulness or pride. Mother kept time with Her hands and joined the others in singing. Some devotees sat in meditation.

Devi Devi Devi Jaganmohini ...

O Goddess, Enchantress of the World,
O Chandika, Slayer of the demons Chanda and Munda,
O Chamundesvari, Divine Mother,
Show us the right path
To cross the ocean of transmigration

The song ended. Amma started talking again. "You should hear Sugunacchan[5] doing japa. It is very interesting. He chants, 'Narayana, Narayana,...,' without stopping for breath, at very high speed." (Everyone laughs as Mother does an imitation.) "The mind will not wander if you chant like that. No one taught him this, he began this himself."

Mother went to Her room, but emerged soon after and paced back and forth in the courtyard. Then She came to the Ashram office and sat down. There were three or four brahmacharis with Her.

The office lacked space. It was a small room. Mother picked up some of the envelopes sitting on a table. They were replies to letters, ready to be mailed.

Mother: "Son, who wrote the addresses on these envelopes? Is this how to write anything? See how carelessly this is

---

[5] Amma's father Sugunanandan

done! Shouldn't the addresses be written neatly even if it takes a little extra time? Or get someone with good handwriting to do it. Who can read it if you write like this, with letters running into each other? This should be done again. A sadhak should do everything with shraddha."

She was about to give the envelopes to a brahmachari. Then She noticed the stamps.

Mother: "What are you children thinking about when you do these things? All these stamps are fixed upside down! This is nothing but carelessness. We can learn about a person's *lakshya bodha* (awareness of the goal) clearly from his actions.

"All of you have come here as seekers of God. You are not going to reach Him without patience and alertness. How will you get concentration in meditation, if you cannot show shraddha in these little things on the gross plane? Meditation is a very subtle thing. It is the shraddha and patience we show in little things that leads us to great achievements.

"Listen to a story. There was a Mahatma. He told his wife that she should always place a glass of water and a needle next to him when he sat down to eat his meals. The wife followed his instructions regularly without asking him about the reason for this. Finally, when the husband became very old and was close to death, he asked her, 'Do you want to ask me anything?' She said, 'There is nothing I need from you, but I would like to know one thing. All these years, I have followed your instructions regularly and placed a glass of water and a needle next to you when you ate. But I never understood what they were for.' The Mahatma replied, 'If a grain of rice were to fall on the floor as you served or as I ate, I wanted to pick it up with the needle, clean it by dipping it in the water and eat it. But because of our alertness, not even a single grain fell on the floor during all these years. Therefore, I didn't have to use the needle and the water.'

"They were careful throughout a whole lifetime not to spill even a single grain of rice while serving or eating. Only those who had shraddha like that have become Mahatmas."

Br: "We will put these letters in new envelopes and mail them, Amma."

Mother: "That would mean wasting these envelopes, son! Where do we have money to waste like that? Don't waste these stamps, either. It is enough to write the addresses neatly on pieces of paper and paste over the old writing. Just be careful from now on."

Mother went to the library next to the office room and sat down on the floor before the brahmacharis got a chance to spread something for Her to sit on. She picked up an illustrated book of stories of the sporting of Krishna. She started looking at each picture carefully. One picture showed Krishna standing with the Govardhana Mountain lifted up on the tip of His little finger. It was raining heavily, and all the cows and cowherds had taken shelter under the mountain.

A brahmachari standing next to Mother saw the picture and asked, "Mother, wasn't Lord Krishna showing a siddhi when He lifted up the Govardhana mountain?"

Mother: "Lord Krishna didn't lift up the mountain to convince others of His power or to earn their respect. That action was necessary under those circumstances. It was raining heavily. There was no other way to protect those who were with Him. So He did what He had to do."

Mother continued after a short silence, "The aim of

Mahatmas is to lead the people to goodness. Countless evil people undergo a change of heart just by getting darshan of a Mahatma."

The lunch bell rang. Mother said, "Children, go and eat now. Amma has some work to do." She went to Her room.

Manasa puja (mental worship)

A brahmachari was waiting for Mother in Her room. He read to Her the article he had written for *Matruvani* (magazine published at the Ashram).

Mother: "Is your meditation going all right, son?"

Br: "I am not getting enough concentration during meditation, Amma."

Mother: "Try practicing *manasa puja* (mental worship), son. Our mind is like a cat. We may take care of it with a lot of affection, but the moment our attention wanders, it will put its head in the pot and steal some food. Manasa puja is a method to keep the wayward mind fixed on God. You should do mental worship, crying out 'Mother, Mother,' with love, devotion and intense yearning. Imagine holding the Divine Mother's hand, and bathing Her by pouring water over Her. Picture the water falling on all parts of Her body and running down. Call out to Her, 'Amma, Amma!' all the while, and visualize Her form. Imagine doing *abhisheka* (ceremonial ablution) one after the other, with milk, honey, *ghee* (clarified butter), sandal paste and rose water. When these things flow down Her body, visualize each part of Her form, from head to foot. Talk to Her and pray to Her. After bathing Her thus, dry Her body with a cloth. Drape a silk sari around Her. Deck Her with ornaments. Put a vermilion mark on Her forehead."

Mother stopped the description and sat in meditation for a long time.

Then she opened Her eyes and continued, "Put anklets on Her. Put a garland on Her neck and enjoy Her beauty. Now do archana with flowers. Take the flower that is your mind, and imagine offering its petals one by one at Her feet. Or imagine offering your vasanas, one by one, in a fire burning in front of Her. After archana, offer Her the payasam of your love. Picture that you are doing arati for Her and see each of Her limbs shining brilliantly in the light of the flame. In the end, imagine that you are circumambulating Mother. All the while, keep praying to Her.

"Try to do with *prema* (devotional love) what Amma just told you, son. Your mind will not wander anywhere."

Mother's words gave new energy to the brahmachari in his path of sadhana. He went out of Her room with a sense of fulfillment, having just seen some of Amma's countless different faces: the all-knowing guru showing the way to Her disciples, the loving Mother, always concerned about the welfare of Her children, the able administrator who runs the affairs of the Ashram with great skill...

Friday, July 5, 1985

It was six in the evening. A teacher and his friend have arrived from Kozhencheri to see Mother. They washed their hands and feet and came inside the kalari and prostrated. The musical instruments for the bhajan were in place. One of the visitors said to the brahmachari who was tuning the tabla, "We started from home this morning, but were late getting here because we were not quite sure of the way. We would like to see Mother and return tonight itself."

Br: "Mother just went to Her room. She was talking to everyone here till now. Perhaps you can see Her when She comes down for the bhajan."

Their faces showed disappointment at having missed Amma's darshan by just a few minutes.

Br: "It may be difficult for you to go back tonight. It is hard to get a bus now. You can see Amma tomorrow and go back easily."

The teacher: "I promised my family that I will get back tonight. They will be worried. If only we could just see Amma… I am sure if we have Her blessings, there won't be any problem."

Br: "How did you hear about Mother?"

Teacher: "The father of one of my students told me about Her. Whenever He talked about Her, his eyes would be brimming with tears. His wife was bedridden for the last four years. She couldn't even get up without help. They tried many treatments, but nothing worked. Last year they came to see Amma. With Her blessings, she recovered completely. My friend told me that he and his wife came here to see Mother even last week."

The brahmachari spread a grass mat for them and said, "You may sit here. If you really must go back tonight, you can prostrate to Amma when She comes for the bhajan and then leave."

Teacher: "My father-in-law visited me the other day. He often goes to hear spiritual discourses. When I talked about

Mother, he asked me whether She was Self-realized. What could I say?"

Br: "The other day I heard someone asking Mother the same question. She said, 'Oh, Amma is just a crazy girl who doesn't know anything!' But the man would not leave it at that. He asked Her again. Finally, Mother said, 'Don't ask a mother of ten whether she has ever given birth to a child!'"

It was time for the bhajan. All the brahmacharis were ready. Mother reached the kalari and the teacher and his friend came forward and prostrated.

Mother put Her hands on their shoulders and said, "Did you just come, children? Amma was down here until a little while ago and went to Her room just for a short time."

Teacher: "We came just when you went to your room, Amma. We are very fortunate to be able to see you now. We have promised to be back home tonight. Otherwise, we would not have minded staying till tomorrow."

Mother: "Do you want to ask me anything, children?" She took them to the verandah of the meditation room. Everyone sat down. The bhajan started in the kalari.

The principles of spiritual life

Teacher: "I have no financial problems, Amma, but I am very worried about my children. I don't get any peace of mind."

Mother: "Son, when your mind is restless, try to chant the mantra. If you seek solace in anything else, all will be lost. If you don't get peace of mind from one thing, you will look for something else. Failing there, you will look for something else again. No peace from anything. Whereas, if you remember

God and chant the mantra, you will achieve tranquillity very quickly. Your mind will get the power to face any situation."

Teacher: "Amma, sometimes I even think of becoming a sannyasin."

Mother: "That is something to be decided on after a lot of thought, son! Sannyasa is not something to sneak away and embrace when you face sorrow. It has to come from your understanding of the ideals. Spiritual life is possible only for someone with a lot of patience. Otherwise only disappointment will be the result. In spiritual life, you need the same kind of discipline and self-restraint as in a prison. But later that prison will be the path to freedom. A sadhak should always be facing towards God. Only then will he be able to reach his goal.

"Many people have asked the children here, 'Why are you living here in the Ashram? Can't you get a job and lead a comfortable life?' They replied, 'We have lived outside, with enough money and all the comforts, but we didn't find peace of mind. But here we get peace and tranquillity without any of that. Through japa and meditation, we are trying to maintain that peace always. Here we have learnt from experience that you get real peace only through remembrance of God. It is that experience that makes us remain in the Ashram.'"

Teacher: "Even though this is our first visit, we have talked to people who come here often. Each of them sees you differently, Amma. Some see you as Devi, some as Krishna, some as their guru. To some, you are the Mother who is the Abode of love and affection. In the eyes of some people, you are just a normal woman. Which of these is the real you, Amma? We would like to know."

Mother: "Each one sees according to his sankalpa, children! The same woman is wife to her husband, mother to her child and sister to her brother. Similarly, isn't a man seen differently by his wife, his mother and his daughter? And the behavior of the same person is not the same towards his mother and his children. The difference is in the concept one has, in the sankalpa. Take a beautiful flower. The bee comes to it for the honey. The poet writes a poem about it. The painter paints a picture. To the worm, it is food. The scientist separates the petals, the pollen and the seed and conducts research on them. The devotee offers it to his deity. Each sees the flower according to his ability and his culture."

Mother continued after a brief pause. "Son, all the labels are given by us. Mother doesn't say that She is a Mahatma or that She is God. Her aim is simply to protect people from the heat of worldly life by bringing them under the umbrella of God; it is to bring about a change, if possible, in the minds of those who are harmful or those who are weak, and make them do good things that benefit themselves and the world. There is no difference in Her mind between those who love Her and those who hate Her."

Teacher: "Some people said that this is a place that leads young people astray."

Mother: "Son, before we voice an opinion about anything, shouldn't we inquire about it, observe it and test it? But, many people now have the habit of passing judgment without knowing or experiencing anything. How can someone who genuinely seeks the truth accept the opinion of such people?

"Many persons, who had only bad habits, reformed completely after coming here. Those who drank regularly gave up alcohol. So how can you say this is a bad place? Why should one give any value to anything that is said, without knowing or experiencing what is going on?

"There are people who are willing to buy a worthless sari at any price if we tell them that it is imported from abroad. They don't value anything made at home, however good it is.

"Someone listens to a song on the radio and says, 'Oh, what a sweet song!' His friend points out that it is the woman living next door who is singing. 'Oh, really? That explains it. It is horrible.' Son, this is human nature. People are losing the ability to look at something, and tell the difference between good and bad. They decide, beforehand, what to see and what to say."

Teacher (pointing to the man accompanying him): "This is a close friend of mine. He is in some serious difficulty. His business is in trouble. He is losing money."

Mother: "Time may not be favorable always, son; there are some bad times. But always remembering God will help alleviate the problems to a large extent."

Teacher: "He does not believe in temples and the like."

Friend: "Mother, God is everywhere, is He not? He is not confined to the four walls of a temple."

Mother: "Don't look at it that way, son. There is wind everywhere; still, we use fans, don't we? Isn't the comfort we get under a shady tree something special? The atmosphere is not the same everywhere. The feeling you get in a temple is not what you get in your office. Don't you feel a special peace and coolness in the temple environment? That is the quality of the atmosphere where remembrance of God takes place constantly.

"Don't think that it is a waste of time to go to the temple.

The children in the first grade need some seeds or marbles to learn how to count. Once they learn it, then there is no need for those things. You can learn swimming easily with the help of a floating log. Once you have learnt well, then you can throw away the log.

"One who has won a prize in long jump may be able to jump several meters. But it will take a lot of practice before children can jump that far. Even with practice, some may not be able to do it. There may be a few Mahatmas who see God in everything; you can count them on your fingers. They don't need temples. But we have to think of all the others. They can reach the Supreme Truth only through such means."

Mother got up saying, "Children, Amma will go for the bhajan now. Both of you stay until the bhajan is over before going home!"

Before they could say anything, Mother walked towards the kalari. She joined the singing. The sweetness of devotion filled the air.

Kannunirillatta kannukalenkilum...

Though my eyes are without tears,
My heart is throbbing with pain.
Though my tongue is silent
It is full of Thy mantra, O Mother!

O mystical tree which fulfills desires,
My mind is always dwelling on thy flowers
But the cruel hunter that is Maya
Is taking aim to cut me down!

You are the auspicious one
Who has come to spread
sandal paste in my soul!
Cool me in the moonlight of your love
and make me fulfilled!

When the arati was over, members of a family approached Mother and prostrated. Their home was in Kozhencheri.

Mother: "Did you come from home today, children?"

Devotee: "We came to visit a relative here in Kayamkulam. We thought we will come to the Ashram before returning home."

Mother: "Wasn't it a month ago that you came here?"

Devotee: "Yes. We couldn't come after that. My father was bedridden with rheumatism."

Mother: "How is he now?"

Devotee: "He is well now. He will come here with us next week."

Mother: "Amma will give you some *prasadam* (ceremonial offering) for him. Are you going home tonight?"

Devotee: "Yes, Amma. My daughter has to work tomorrow."

Mother: "But how will you go this late at night?"

Devotee: "We have come in a jeep."

Mother: "Oh, then there are two other children here who have come from there. They wanted to go back earlier. Mother asked them to stay for the bhajan."

Devotee: "There is no problem. There is plenty of room in the jeep. We are only three."

Mother introduced the teacher and his friend to them. The teacher said, "We were about to leave soon after seeing

Mother. When She asked us to stay till the bhajan was over, we worried that the last bus would be gone. Now we know that our problems will be gone if we put our trust fully in Mother."

Mother asked a brahmacharini to bring *vibhuti* (holy ash). Amma gave some of it to everyone as prasadam. She gave a special portion for the devotee's father. She returned to Her room after instructing a brahmacharini to see that everyone had supper.

Monday, July 8, 1985

It was five in the afternoon. Mother was sitting in the kalari. The brahmachari who had gone to buy vegetables in town came back with the packages. A sack full of rice was on his head. On his shoulder, he carried a bag of vegetables. It was clear that he was carrying more than he could comfortably carry.

Seeing his difficulty, Mother took the sack of rice from his head and put it down. She asked: "Did you go alone when you had all these things to buy? Couldn't you take someone with you?"

Br: "I didn't think it would be this heavy." Two brahmacharis took the bags to the kitchen.

Mother: "Of course. How can you tell how heavy your purchases are without doing some work at home or lifting some load? How did you lift the sack of rice to your head?"

Br: "The man running the ferry helped."

Mother: "Poor son! From now on, don't go to the market alone." She ran Her fingers over his head. The son stood there enjoying this loving caress from Amma, blissfully forgetting everything else.

The happiness and sorrow of worldly life

Mother came back to the kalari and sat down. A woman came near and prostrated. Mother gave her an embrace, holding Her close. The woman put her head in Mother's lap and started sobbing. 'If only Amma makes a sankalpa, all my troubles will be over,' she kept saying. Mother patted her on the back and consoled her.

Mother: "Daughter, is it enough if Mother makes a sankalpa? You should become ready to accept it. Even if Mother turns on the light, you have to open the door before the light can get in. If all the doors are closed tightly, how can you get light? Even when Amma makes a resolve, for it to benefit you, you have to think of God, daughter. You should set apart some time for chanting God's name every day. How much time we waste daily! Is it enough to say that Amma should make everything all right, when you are not making any effort?"

The woman believed that all her troubles arose from the evil spells cast by her neighbors. She was trying to convince Mother of this. She wanted Mother to punish her neighbors and to protect her. She had repeated this demand several times by now. Mother's voice became stern when it was clear that the woman was not paying attention to Her persuasion. The woman stopped complaining and began listening to Mother with fear and reverence.

Mother: "We have two kinds of happiness and sorrow now. When we don't get what we want, we are sorry; but when others get what they wish, our sorrow is even greater. Similarly we are happy when we succeed in something, but we are happier when others suffer from failure. We forget all our sorrows and rejoice when we see the sorrow of others. Our own girl may be unmarried, but we are happy that the neighbor's daughter is unmarried also, and we become sad when her wedding takes place. Children, this is a depravity of the mind. It is a serious disease that eats away our peace. It is a cancer of the mind.

"Once two neighbors went to buy timber. One of them bought one log while the other bought three. When the first one cut his log, he found it to be hollow inside. He was very unhappy at having wasted his money and he couldn't even eat because of this. Then his wife came with the news that all three of the neighbor's logs were rotten inside. The man who was stricken with grief until then suddenly got a burst of joy. 'O really! Get me some tea!' he says, laughing happily, 'He deserves it. It is only fair. He thinks he is so rich, and went and bought three of them! He deserves it.'

"Children, the first thing we should do is to change this attitude. When our mind is like this, no amount of japa will benefit us. We will not get God's grace or peace of mind. We should clean a pot that held sour things thoroughly before putting milk in it. Otherwise, the milk will go bad. Children, our first prayer should be to get a heart that rejoices in the happiness of others and shares their sorrow.

"If our next door neighbor is crazy, we also have some problems. We will not be able to sleep because of the noise he makes at night. We may not have peace even during the day. Think of the unhappiness we face if our brother comes home drunk every day and starts a fight. Our peace will be completely lost. If the brother is good-natured, we all share the peace. When others lead a life of peace and quiet, we should realize that we are the ones who benefit from it. At least, we are not getting any troubles from them! We should be able to rejoice in their happiness and feel compassion in their sorrow. That means we are growing in our hearts. It is in such hearts that God likes to reside. God's real children are those who see the happiness and sorrow of others as their own."

The woman had started crying by then, and Mother paused to wipe her tears. "Don't feel bad, daughter. Regularly chant the mantra that Mother gave you. Everything will be all right."

The woman was consoled by this. She prostrated and got up. She said good bye after thus unloading her burden of sorrows in front of the Mother, who is the refuge of all those who suffer. Aren't we sure to get solace if we bathe in that stream of unbroken peace that flows towards all grieving hearts?

Saturday, July 20, 1985

No compromise in the discipline

The brahmacharis are doing archana in the meditation room. Mother is pacing back and forth on the verandah. There is great seriousness in Her as She walked with Her hands held together in the back. It is not quite daybreak yet. Two men with flashlights pass by the banks of the canal on the southern side of the Ashram. They must be fishermen getting ready to cast their net.

A brahmachari came running to join the archana. He must have been a little late getting up. He gently opened the door of the meditation room to go in. Mother stopped him by reaching out and closing the door tightly. The brahmachari stood near the door with bowed head. Mother said after a few minutes:

"Don't you know that the archana starts at five in the morning? If people come in one by one after it starts, everyone doing the archana will lose concentration. You stay outside and do the archana today. From tomorrow onwards, you should be in the meditation room by four thirty. You should adhere to a discipline in sadhana - then only will you make any progress.

The brahmachari put his seat on the verandah and sat down. The mantras resounded within the meditation room. The meaning of each mantra became clear as he fixed his mind on the holy feet of the Mother who was pacing in front with gentle steps.

> *Om nakhadhiditisamchanna namajjana tamogunayai namah...*
>
> *Salutations to Her, whose radiant toenails dispel the ignorance of the devotees who prostrate in front of Her!*
>
> *Salutations to Her whose feet defeat lotus flowers in radiance!*
>
> *Salutations to Her whose auspicious lotus feet are adorned with gem-studded golden anklets*
> *that twinkle sweetly.*
>
> *Salutations to Her whose gait is as slow and gentle as that of a swan!*

The brahmacharis who emerged after the archana were pleasantly surprised to see Mother there and they all prostrated.

Mother put her hands on the head of the son who had arrived late and blessed him.

Mother: "Son, were you sad when Amma stopped you from going in to join the archana?"

What pain is there when one's heart melts in Mother's love as the *chandrakanta*[6] stone melts in the light of the full moon?

Mother: "This is an ashram, son. When we do archana at the *brahma muhurta* (the sacred hour before dawn) all the children should take part in it. At that time there shouldn't be anyone sleeping or bathing. Everyone should be seated five minutes before the archana starts."

Br: "There was only a trickle of water coming out of the pipe. So I was late by the time I finished my bath."

Mother: "If you have an examination or a job interview, will you children say you were late because there was no water or electricity? You should do your sadhana with the same attitude.

"When so many of you are doing the archana together, the Divine Mother is definitely present here. One shouldn't walk in or talk or sleep at that time. That is why Amma told you to do the archana outside, as they had already started inside."

Mother caressed all Her children with Her loving eyes and went to Her room. She emerged again at seven o'clock with a brahmacharini and started walking on the grounds on the north side. She gathered together the coconut leaves that

---

[6] The chandrakanta stone is said to melt away under the influence of the moon.

had fallen there. A brahmachari took it all to the side of the kitchen. He did not waste the opportunity to clear some of his doubts by asking Mother a question directly.

Br: "Mother, can one eliminate the mind completely?"

Mother: "Son, mind means a collection of thoughts. Thoughts are like the waves in the ocean. They will keep rising up one after another. One cannot stop the waves by force. But when the ocean is deep, the waves subside. Similarly, try to concentrate the mind on one thought, instead of trying to stop all thoughts by force. Then the ocean of the mind will become deeper. It will become quiet. Even if there are small waves on the surface, it will be peaceful below."

Mother's cow seva

Mother reached the side of the cowshed. A brahmachari was washing a cow. It was a newly-purchased cow. She was called Shantini (the peaceful one). But there was no connection between her name and her behavior. So far, no one who tried to bathe her had escaped without getting at least one lash with her tail. It took three people to milk her, and her feet had to be tied. It was like a battle. It was as if she had taken a vow to see that the milk ended up on the ground, or that at least those who had tried to milk her would get a milk bath.

The brahmachari who knew Shantini's nature well, was pouring water over her using a cup. He wetted her body twice and called it her bath. The dirt and dung were still sticking to her body. Mother did not like this way of washing the cow. She took the bucket of water from the brahmachari. The brahmachari went to the kitchen and got a piece of the rough outer husk of a coconut. Mother showed Her son how to wash the cow. Very carefully, She removed the dung that was sticking to the belly and the legs of the cow and washed her clean.

Everyone was surprised at the docility of Shantini, which was never seen in her before. She stood there like a very obedient child. Perhaps she had waited all this time for such an occasion!

As Mother was bathing the cow She said: "Son, don't stand behind a cow when you wash her. She may kick. This one is a bit unruly, so you have to wash her carefully, standing on the sides." She also showed how the cow should be tethered in the cowshed.

Hearing that Amma was washing the cow, two devotees came to see it. As She came out of the cowshed, Mother said to them: "The children here are not used to doing any of this. They have come here straight out of college. These are children who have been pampered by their parents. They don't know how to wash their own clothes. Yesterday Mother saw one of them trying to use 'Superwhite' (a blue dye) while washing his clothes. It would have been great fun if Mother hadn't gotten there just then! He took just half a bucket of water and emptied a whole bottle of 'Superwhite' into it. When Amma got there, he was just going to dip his white clothes in it. Imagine what would have happened! (She laughs.) He finished a whole month's supply of 'Superwhite' in just one washing. Mother showed him how to mix a drop of dye in a bucket of water and to dip the clothes in it."

Advice to householders

Mother sat on the verandah of the meditation room. The devotees sat on the ground near Her. Mr. Menon from Palakkad started the conversation.

Menon: "Mother, I practice some meditation. Because of various problems, I am never free from sorrow. I have talked to many householders like myself. Most of them are in the same situation. I even wonder sometimes why one does japa and meditation."

Mother: "Son, just doing japa and meditation is not enough. One should assimilate the basic principles. When Mother was young, She used to cut the branches of a *kampatti*[7] tree. She would climb up the tree. The first time She did it, She got burnt throughout Her body. Her face was so swollen She couldn't see anything. It took two or three days for Her to become normal again. Then She heard that one should rub oil on the body before doing this. After that, She would always use the protection of oil when breaking the branches of the *kampatti*. Similarly, you should apply the oil that is love for God before entering family life. Then there will be no cause for sorrow.

"One should have the conviction that God is one's real relative. Children, you should know that all the other relations and worldly things will only give sorrow eventually. Maintain a relation only to God within you. This does not mean that you should abandon your wife and children, or that you should see them as strangers. You should take care of them well. But, know that the only lasting relative you have is God. All the

---

[7] A tree whose sap burns the skin.

others will leave you today or tomorrow. Therefore, always take refuge in Him. Think that difficulties in life are for your good. Then there will be peace and tranquillity in family life."

A devotee: "Can we live like those who do great tapas?"

Mother: "Mother is not saying that householders should undertake severe austerities, but try to chant the holy name while you perform any action. There is no need to worry about the purity of the body while chanting. The Lord is everywhere. He is always in our hearts. It is just that we don't know it. A diamond has a natural brightness; but when it falls into oil it loses its shine. Similarly, we are not able to recognize Him because of ignorance. In the morning, you should chant the holy name for at least ten minutes after your bath. Meditate at least for a little while. You should do the same thing in the evening. Whoever causes you grief, take your complaints to the puja room. Our real friend is there. Choose a friend in addition to your husband or wife - that should be the Lord. Even if your unhappiness arises from your husband or wife, tell it to God without telling anyone else. If your neighbor picks a fight with you, go to the puja room and complain, 'Why did You let them abuse me like that? Weren't You with me?' Open your hearts and tell Him everything. Then it becomes a satsang. When someone gives you something good, tell God about it also.

"If we forget God in times of happiness and remember Him only in times of sorrow, it is not a sign of true devotion. We should remember him always.

"Any spare time you get after work should be spent in reading spiritual books like the *Gita* and *Ramayana* or biographies or collections of the teachings of Mahatmas - and not in going to the movies. Don't waste any opportunity to participate in satsangs. Share with your friends the things you hear in satsangs, thus bringing mental peace to them also. Observe brahmacharya at least two or three days in a week. That is essential for getting the proper benefit out of sadhana. (Laughing) There is not just one wife - the eyes, nose, tongue, ears and the skin are all our 'wives' - we have to control our attachment to them also. Only then can we know the real essence in us."

A female devotee: "Amma, where is the time for satsang and reading after finishing the household chores and taking care of the children?"

Mother: "Those who want it will have time. Even those who repeat a hundred times that they have no time will rush a sick child to the hospital, won't they? Even if it takes three or four months for treatment, they won't leave the hospital and go to work. Even if you complain many times about lack of time, when it comes to the health of your child, you find time. Similarly, when you are convinced that God is the One who protects you and that there will not be peace in this life without taking refuge in Him, then you will find time for it.

"If you cannot find free time to devote to the worship of God, try to be like the *gopis*. They did not set apart a separate time for prayer. They saw God while immersed in their work. They would repeat the holy name while churning the milk and grinding the grain and in all their other chores. The jars of pepper and coriander and all the other spices were labeled with the name of the Lord. When they wanted pepper they asked for Mukunda. When they gave coriander to someone, they were giving Govinda. Those who came for milk and curd asked for them using the Lord's names. They were engaged in nothing but chanting Krishna's names everywhere and at all times. Thus they were able to remember the Lord always, without any special effort. Those who are not able to set apart a special time for sadhana can still maintain remembrance of God in this way.

"One should firmly fix in mind the idea that only God is true and eternal. One should practice chanting the mantra while engaged in work. Then there won't be any need for a special time for remembering God. Our minds will always stay in Him."

Devotee: "Is it not enough to contemplate on the Self? Is it necessary to chant the mantra and so forth?"

Mother: "Son, school children are asked to repeat poems and the multiplication table to commit them to memory. One reading may not be enough for everyone to memorize such things. Similarly it will not be possible for everyone to fix the mind in the Supreme Principle just through contemplation, without doing japa or singing hymns in solitude. If someone is able to do it through contemplation, then he needs only that; there is no need for anything else. But, when you chant the mantra or sing kirtans, your mind becomes one-pointed quickly. It won't run to external things as easily as at other times. This is something that everyone can do."

The devotees who were arriving at the Ashram began to gather to enjoy the sweetness of Mother's words. When their number became quite large, Mother went to the hut to start giving darshan.

A young woman who had lost her mental balance was brought in by her parents. Seeing their sorrow, Mother gave them permission to stay in the Ashram for a few days.

Someone had to be with the girl at all times. If no one watched, she would run away. Someone always held her hand. Mother gave a piece of sandalwood to the father and asked him to apply sandalwood paste to the girl's forehead frequently.

The bhajan was over. As Mother sat in the courtyard in front of the kalari along with the devotees and the brahmacharis, the sick girl got out of her room and started running off. Her mother and sister followed her. A brahmacharini and another woman ran after the girl and somehow caught her and brought her back. Mother made her sit nearby. The girl kept asking Mother meaningless questions. Mother listened to her with attention and soothed her by answering occasionally.

On Mother's instruction, the girl was taken near the water tap outside the meditation room. Amma filled a bucket with water and poured it in an unbroken stream on the girl's head. She repeated this several times. She held the girl's hand tightly to stop her from running away. This continued for about half an hour. By that time there was a slight change in the girl's behavior. Mother made some sandal paste and applied it to the girl's forehead. Before sending her to her room with her mother, Amma did not forget to bestow an affectionate kiss on the girl's cheek.

Mother came back and sat down in the yard in front of the kalari. She called Br. Balu and asked him to sing a kirtan. Br. Sri Kumar played the harmonium. The Ashram air filled with blissful devotional music.

Sri chakram ennoru chakram...

In the mystical wheel Sri Chakram
Dwells the Goddess Sri Vidya

That Devi, who is the nature of motion,
The one Power that moves the wheel of the Universe

Sometimes riding on a lion,
Sometimes mounted on a swan,
Manifesting as the Shakti of Lord Brahma[8],
O Mother who leads and controls
The Divine Trinity,
Is not the Goddess Katyayani
Yet another of Thy forms?

These devotees pay obeisance to Thy forms
For the alleviation of their miseries.
O Mother, who among the human beings,
Captivated by Maya, understands the truth
That this human body is most despicable?

O Mother, Thou who sports riding on a tiger,
How can one in ignorance hope to extol
Thy most exalted majesty?

Tuesday, August 6, 1985

Mother came down the steps of Her room, dressed in pure white. All the devotees who were waiting for Her with joined palms started softly chanting 'Amma, Amma.' Mother walked to the kalari accompanied by all Her children. There was not enough room inside for everyone. Those who did not get a seat inside, waited outside for their turn. Mother's broad smile soothed everyone. Her compassionate eyes brought relief to aching hearts.

---
[8] This is a reference to Saraswati, the consort of Lord Brahma.

A young woman put her head in Mother's lap and sobbed. Amma raised her head and wiped her tears affectionately. She tried to console the young woman saying, "Don't cry, daughter! Amma is here for you! Don't cry!" But she continued to weep, unable to control her sorrow. Mother pulled her close and caressed her back with love.

The young woman came from a rich family. She fell in love with one of her brother's friends. The family opposed this as the young man belonged to a different caste. But their love prevailed and they got married. They rented a house and started their life together. The husband borrowed some money and started a business. The venture failed. The pressure from his creditors grew very intense. He left home without telling anyone.

"Amma, he has abandoned me and the children. We have no one to look after us!" The woman kept repeating this as she cried on Mother's shoulder.

Mother tried to console her again. "Stop worrying, my daughter. Nothing has happened to him. He will come back."

The young woman raised her head from Mother's shoulder and asked, "Will my husband come back, Amma?"

Mother: "Surely. He will be back. Don't worry, daughter!" After a brief silence, Mother continued, "Amma will give you a mantra. Keep Devi in your mind always and chant the mantra regularly. All your problems will be gone in a month's time."

The woman's face brightened. Hopeful expectation gleamed in her eyes. Mother closed Her eyes and sat in meditation for a little while. Then She opened Her eyes again, chanting 'Shiva, Shiva!'

Mother's divine mood of bhakti

One by one, the devotees prostrated in front of Mother and withdrew. Mr. Bhaskaran Nair from Thrissur came forward and prostrated. Since his wife's death, he spends all his time in spiritual pursuits. He came to the Ashram frequently to see Mother. The peace that was evident on his face, his humility and the mala of *tulasi* (basil) beads around his neck all spoke of his *sattvic* (serene) nature.

Amma opened the packet that Mr. Nair offered Her. It contained a picture and a biography of Chaitanya Mahaprabhu. Mother looked the book over. She then opened it and handed it to Mr. Nair, saying: "You read a little, son! Amma will listen." He was very pleased and started reading:

"Once love for the Lord begins to blossom in your heart, then no other thought will enter. Will the tongue that has tasted rock candy yearn for the sweetness of other worthless things? The blessed soul who has developed love for God constantly becomes intoxicated by it. The lover pines every second to be united with his beloved. He does not worry at all whether his beloved loves him back or not. Every moment he will be thinking of his dear beloved and be brooding over the separation. Mahaprabhu's love was of this kind. The stream of prema that issued from the lake of his heart grew stronger and stronger. That *Ganga* (Ganges river) of love never dried up as little streams did. One moment he would laugh, the next moment he would dance. He would drench his clothes in tears all night without sleeping. He would sigh deeply, calling out 'Oh Krishna, Oh Krishna!' Mahaprabhu became incapable of performing the normal routine actions such as bathing, offering his twilight-prayers or eating. He could not talk about or hear about anything but the exploits of Krishna. He knew none other than his ever beloved Krishna."

Mr. Nair glanced at Amma as he was reading. She had become completely oblivious of the world. Her eyes closed slowly. The radiance of Her divine face seemed to fill the surroundings. Tears drops rolled halfway down Her cheeks and stopped. The divine mood of bhakti in Mother spread to the devotees around Her. Everyone sat still, watching Her with unblinking eyes. One woman wept, crying out 'Amma, Amma!' loudly. Madhavan Nair stopped reading and, with palms joined in devotion, sat watching Amma's divine face intently. Overcome by devotion, one woman started singing *Ayi! giri nandini nandita mohini...*

> *O Daughter of the Mountain! Enchantress,*
> *Worshipped by all, worshipped by Nandi,*
> *You who sports with the universe,*
> *You who resides on Mount Vindhya,*
> *O Goddess who is the wife of Shiva,*
> *You with a large family, You who have done*
> *Many wondrous deeds, Victory to You,*
> *O slayer of the demon Mahisha,*
> *Beautiful beloved of Shiva,*
> *Daughter of Himavat!*

Mother opened Her eyes after about an hour and a half. After giving darshan to the devotees, She went and sat down in the shade between the Vedanta school and the hut. Some brahmacharis and a few others were around Her. One of them was Surendran who sold liquor earlier in his life. After meeting

Mother, he stopped that work. Now he runs a general store next to his house.

The past is a cancelled check

Surendran: "Amma, I have made many mistakes in my life. Their memories are bothering me a lot now."

Mother: "Son, why are you worrying about past mistakes? What is past is past. If you fret about them, you will lose whatever strength you have now. Make a firm decision that you will not make such mistakes again. That is what is needed. Then, your pure actions will cleanse your mind. Your desire to be good in thought and action and your effort in that direction show the purity of your mind. You didn't know at the time of your earlier actions that they were wrong. Now that you know they were wrong, you are trying to turn away from them. That is enough. When a child throws a ball at his mother, she will only smile. She will pick up the child and kiss it. But after growing up, if he hurls something at her, she will not forgive that. Similarly, we have done many wrong things until now without realizing it. God will forgive them all. But He will not forgive the mistakes we make after we know that they are wrong. Therefore, our effort should be to avoid repeating our mistakes.

"There is no need to feel sorry about the way we lived till now. That is like a canceled check. Or, it is like the errors you make when you write. You have the pencil and the eraser. You can erase your mistakes, but you can do it only a couple of times. If you erase too many times, you will tear the paper. The Lord will forget the errors that we make unknowingly. The biggest error is to repeat something that we know is wrong. That we shouldn't do."

Devotee: "Do I deserve to pray to God, Mother? Do I have the purity of mind for that?"

Mother: "Don't think like that, son! Don't think that you lack the mental purity to pray now because you have made mistakes in your life and that you will pray when your mind gets pure. If you think that you will bathe in the sea after the waves subside, you will never be able to bathe. You can't learn to swim by sitting on the side of the pool. You have to get into the water. What will happen if a doctor tells the patient to come to him only after he gets well? The Lord is the One who purifies our minds. That is why we take refuge in Him. Only through Him we can cleanse ourselves."

Surendran: "Amma, once we have faith in You and devotion for You, we can't do anything wrong. Therefore, we only ask for Your grace so that we will have faith and devotion."

Mother: "Children, it is enough if you have faith in God. If you have firm faith in Him, you will not make mistakes. There will be only happiness in your lives."

Surendran: "Are you not God, Yourself, Amma?"

Mother: "Amma does not like to say that. Suppose a fragrant flower blossoms on a plant. The plant shouldn't say, 'Look at my flower! How beautiful, how fragrant! That comes from my power.' If it says so, it is feeding the ego. All powers belong to God. We should never think that anything is ours. None of this is due to Amma's power. She blossomed because of His power. He endued Her with fragrance. Mother will not say that any of this is Hers."

The cause of sorrow and the remedy

A devotee: "Mother, what is the reason for sorrow?"

Mother: "The attitude of 'I' and 'mine' is the reason for all sorrow.

Once we were coming back from Kozhikode. There was a householder son on the bus, with his child. He sat in his seat, playing with the child. After a while, the father fell asleep. The child also fell asleep in the father's lap, but slipped and fell to the floor a little later. The father didn't know this. He woke up only when the child began to cry. Then he, too, began to weep, saying, 'O my son, my son!' He started to look for possible signs of injury to the child. Thus, his attitude of 'I' and 'mine' turned into sorrow as soon as he woke up. If that attitude is absent, there is no sorrow.

"Two young boys were playing with a stick. A third child saw this and started crying for a stick for himself. When he made a fuss, his mother came and took the stick from the other boys and gave it to him. He started playing with it, but soon he fell asleep. The stick slipped from his hand. He didn't even know. He had cried for it only a little while before. But in his sleep, he lost the attitude of 'I' and 'mine.' That made him calm and he could sleep peacefully, forgetting everything. Similarly, when our self resides in Brahman, it is bliss. If we give up the attitude of 'I' and 'mine,' we can enjoy that bliss. Then there is no more sorrow. But we do have to give up the attitude of 'I' as an individual."

Devotee: "Mother, is it that easy for everyone?"

Mother: "Try, my son! We may not climb a mountain, but can't we at least pick up a handful of sand from it? If we remove a handful of water from the ocean, there will be that much less remaining. Just think of it in that way. If you have complete dedication and put forth constant effort, anything becomes possible. If you keep pouring water into a bottle of ink, won't the color slowly fade until finally you can't tell whether there was any ink at all to begin with? In the same way, as the mind expands with constant remembrance of God, the sense of individuality slowly shrinks and finally disappears. The individual mind becomes the universal mind."

Another devotee: "Amma, many people hate me just because I have money. Is it wrong to acquire wealth?"

Mother: "Children, it is not wrong to have money. But one's life shouldn't be just for amassing money. One may save money for one's needs, but not in excess.

"Once there was an umbrella maker in a village. As he worked, he chanted God's name and engaged in satsang with those who came to him. He lived happily, contented with what he earned and everyone liked him. He earned enough daily to meet his needs adequately.

"One day a land owner bought an umbrella from him. Pleased with the high quality and moderate price of the umbrella, the land owner took a special interest in the umbrella maker whose good qualities attracted him. The land owner gave him some money as gift. As soon as he got the money, the umbrella maker's character changed. His mind no longer stayed on the job. 'How will I protect the money? Is it safe to keep it at home? Or will it be stolen?' He began to worry like this. As these thoughts about money arose, the japa stopped. He couldn't finish his work on time. His thoughts were on future plans: should he build a house or should he start a larger business? These were his only thoughts. Because of this he didn't pay attention to his work. He came to dislike talking to others. He forgot how to speak with love. He was annoyed at anyone asking him anything, as it disturbed his thoughts. Fewer and fewer people came to his store now. His income plummeted. The thoughts about money robbed his peace of mind. As his greed and selfishness increased, he became restless and full of sorrow. Soon the money he received as a gift was all gone. He had no more work. The man who had led a contented life before he got the money, had only torment now.

"Children, when we go to an excess in anything, it will bring an end to peace. Therefore, always try to lead a simple life. That alone is enough to bring us mental peace. We don't need anything in excess."

How simple is the style Amma uses to remove doubts from the minds of Her children! Their minds yearn to hear, again and again, those nectar-filled words which impart knowledge through simple stories and examples containing priceless gems of wisdom. They would pray in their minds as Arjuna prayed to Krishna, 'I have not heard enough of this nectar! Please let me hear more and more!'

CHAPTER THREE

Wednesday, August 7, 1985

Mother was sitting at a level spot on the bank of the canal that ran by the side of the Ashram. She sat facing the water. All the brahmacharis came and sat around Her for meditation. The atmosphere was a peaceful and solemn one which made the mind naturally introspective. It seemed that even the waves in the ocean had subsided. Everyone tried to enter into meditation. Mother cast Her compassionate glance at everyone and said slowly:

Meditation

"Children, when you sit for meditation, do not think that you can arrest your mind immediately. At first, you should relax all parts of your body. Loosen your clothes if they are too tight. Make sure that the spine is erect. Then close your eyes and concentrate your mind on your breath. You should be aware of your inhalation and exhalation. Normally we breath in and out without being aware of it. It should not be like that. One should become aware of the process. Then the mind would be wakeful. As you sit like that for a while, your minds will become calm. You can continue the meditation by concentrating attention on your breath. Or you can start meditating on the form of your beloved deity. If the mind wanders, you should bring it back. If you are unable to do that, then it is enough to watch where it is going. The mind should be kept under observation. Then it will stop running around and come under our control.

"Start meditating now, children!"

She who removes all dangers

All the brahmacharis became engrossed in meditation. Mother abruptly woke up from meditation. Seeing the unusual change in Her mood, a brahmacharis enquired the reason.

Mother: "Son, something has happened to one of the children." She paused for a while. Then She continued, "That *mon* who comes regularly from Kozhencheri, it was him that Amma saw. Amma had told him when he was here last week that he should be careful while traveling in vehicles. She had told him specially not to drive any vehicles for three months."

Mother appeared particularly worried. She returned to Her room quickly.

Amma's words reminded Haridas, a devotee from Pattambi, of what had happened to him a year before. He described the incident. "I used to come with my family in my jeep to see Amma. One day when I was here, She told me, 'Don't drive for some time, son! Amma sees darkness ahead!' So, on the return trip, I made my brother drive the jeep. Two months later, my brother and I went to Sultan Battery to visit a friend. When we got there, my brother developed some stomach trouble. He was not in a position to drive or even to travel. I had to be back home by next morning because of some financial matters and so I couldn't stay there. I left my brother in my friend's home and left that night itself.

"Since I remembered Amma's words, I was driving slowly and very carefully. I was chanting Her mantra. On the way, I felt sleepy. I stopped for a cup of tea. I washed my face with cold water and then continued my journey. But after driving a little bit, I felt sleepy again. I was struggling to stay awake while driving. Finally I dozed off for a moment. The jeep got out of control and swerved to the right. Suddenly I felt that someone had grabbed the steering wheel and turned it to the left. That same instant I called out 'Amma' and applied the brakes. The jeep came to a stop, almost touching a rock on the left side of the road. It was not possible to see anything very clearly in the darkness. It was a road built on the side of a mountain. The rising mountain on the left, and a very deep valley on the right. Only when I saw that the jeep had stopped close to the edge of the road to the left that I was convinced that the help of the unseen rescuer was not just my imagination.

"I came to the ashram the next week itself. As soon as She saw me Mother asked, 'Son, did you drive, even though Mother told you not to?' I could only stand there with tears in my eyes."

Amma protects Her children, just like a mother who guards her babies, holding them in her arms, never putting them down. She knows every one of their thoughts and every breath they take.

Is the future predestined?

Mother came down from Her room only after the bhajan was over. A family had come from Bhopal to see Her. They were visiting their hometown in Kerala on vacation. There they heard about Mother and wanted to see Her. They had just a week left before returning to Bhopal. The head of the family had absorbed spiritual principles from his father who was a firm devotee of Sri Ramakrishna. The wife and children also had deep faith in God. They always found time for sadhana in the midst of their busy life. They were planning to return home after getting Mother's darshan that night itself. As they had their own car, returning late at night was no problem.

When he got a chance to speak to Mother, the devotee said: "Amma, life's troubles have increased a lot recently. My wife was in the hospital for a month. When she came home, our son fell ill. He was also in the hospital for a week. My wife says that our troubles will disappear if we get our horoscopes examined and do whatever remedies are suggested."

Mother: "Is there someone near you who can study your horoscopes?"

Devotee: "My wife's father knows astrology. She makes a fuss everyday about this. She wants to send everybody's horoscope to him. I have no faith at all in horoscopes and such things, Amma! We have to go through whatever is destined to happen. So why go through all this?"

Mother: "It is not right to say that there is no meaning in all this. We can know our future to some extent by studying the planetary positions. If we know the path ahead of us, we can avoid troubles. Can't we avoid a thorny fence or a ditch on the way ahead, if we know that they are there?"

Devotee: "Can we change destiny, then?"

Mother: "Destiny can be changed through tapas and sadhana. Even death can be averted. Don't you know the story of the sage, Markandeya? Didn't his fate change, as his heart cried out in prayer when he faced death?

"Anything in our fate can be transcended by performing actions fully surrendered to God. But we have to be ready to act, in stead of sitting somewhere idly blaming fate. It is a sign laziness to blame fate without doing any work."

Devotee: "Then the horoscope that foretells the future would turn out to be wrong, won't it?"

Mother: "Son, one's effort will surely make a difference. Amma will tell you a story. Two friends got their horoscopes written. It turned out that both of them were going to be killed by snakebite according to their horoscopes. One of them began to worry about this constantly. His constant anxiety made him mentally sick. His family also lost their peace of mind. The other man did not fall a prey to anxiety. He thought about a possible solution. He became aware of the limits of his abilities, and he became a devotee of God. He surrendered himself to God. Still, using the healthy body and intelligence that God had given him, he took all the precautions he could to avoid being bitten by snakes. He stayed at home always remembering God.

"One night as he went into his puja room in the dark, his foot hit something. In the room, there was an idol of a snake, with its tongue protruding. That was what his foot touched - at the hour he was supposed to be bitten by a snake, according to the horoscope. Even though it was a lifeless snake, he was injured. There was no poison, however. The effort he made with dedication to God became fruitful. His friend, on the other hand, became a victim of anxiety before anything happened and he wasted his life. Lead a life of self-effort, son, without blaming fate! All obstacles can be overcome that way."

Devotee: "Mother, I have a doubt."

Mother: "What is it, son!"

Devotee: "If fate could be changed, couldn't Sri Krishna change Duryodhana's mind and avoid war? Would Duryodhana have gone to war, If Krishna had revealed his divine form to him?"

Mother: "The Lord showed His supreme form to both the Pandavas and the Kauravas. Because of his humility, Arjuna could recognize the Lord's greatness. The egoistic Duryodhana could not. There is no use showing anything to those who don't have an attitude of surrender. Spiritual principles can be imparted only to someone who deserves it and who is of the right conduct. Realization of the body was what Duryodhana considered important! He didn't have the attitude to absorb the Lord's advice. His view was that whatever Krishna said was not for his good, but was meant to help the Pandavas. Whatever Krishna told him, he would take it in the opposite sense. Only through war the ego of such persons can be destroyed."

The Holy Mother's face took on a serious expression. Suddenly She got up; Her thoughts had shifted to something else. The family of devotees prostrated and withdrew. Mother walked to the coconut grove. She started pacing alone there. She was singing the lines of a hymn in a low voice. She raised both Her arms towards the sky and sang the same verse again and again with feeling, Her voice breaking and faltering.

After a while, Mother sat down in the sand, looking down. Was She shedding tears for Her children? No one dared to break that solitude. Everyone slipped away gently. Mother lay down in the sand. She remained in that position for several hours. Man's feeble mind retreats in defeat when it tries to understand the unfathomable nature of Amma's actions. Total surrender is the only course left to it!

Saturday, August 10, 1985

The day was just breaking. During the night, a middle-aged man had arrived at the ashram, too drunk to walk erectly. Two young men were now haggling with him for the money he owed them. He had hired their auto-rikshaw at night to come to the ashram. Along the way, he had stopped at all the liquor shops. By the time they reached here, he had no money left. They were asking for sixty rupees. He had just a few coins. Finally he gave them his expensive watch and sent them away.

He walked with unsteady steps. The brahmacharis helped him to the verandah of the Vedanta school and made him lie down. Following a devotee's advice, he was made to drink some buttermilk. Someone helped him change his clothes.

It was eight in the morning. In the ashram center at Kollam, there was going to be a program of archana and bhajan today in Mother's divine presence. She came down from Her room, ready to start on the journey. The man who had arrived totally drunk earlier, now ran towards Amma. He had bathed meanwhile and covered himself with sacred ash. He prostrated fully in front of Amma and recited aloud hymns to the Divine Mother. In between, he let Amma know of his troubles. Even though She knew about his drinking, She consoled him with tender motherly love. She said, "Amma will return tonight. Stay here tonight, son! Yon can go back after *bhava darshan* tomorrow."

Some devotees were also going on the trip to Kollam with Amma and the brahmacharis. She got into the canoe that served as ferry across the backwater. Anxious to be with Her, everyone got into the same boat. There were too many people. Mother who does not like to see any of Her children unhappy, did not ask any one to get down. If the canoe tipped a little water would get in. If a motor boat were to pass by, the canoe would certainly sink in its wake. Every body was very confident that nothing untoward would happen as Amma was with them.

"Children, there are some here who don't know how to swim. So, be very careful, everybody! If you stir, the boat will go down," She said very gravely. The boat gently moved away from the shore.

The spiritual journey

Mother said: "Children, the spiritual journey is just like this trip. We have to sit with self-control, even holding our breath, till we get down on the other shore. The boat may sink if we don't have that kind of control. In the same way, until we get to the other shore of the ocean of samsara, until we attain *purnam* ('completeness') there, we have to take each step very carefully. Once we are there, there are no more worries."

Amma sat on the wooden board in the canoe that served as a seat, with Her eyes cast on the water. And when Mother is with Her children, holding their hands firmly, what is there to be afraid of! Every one was free of anxiety.

They all boarded the bus on the other side. During the trip, Br. Venu said to Amma: "Recently a devotee told me that he had no faith in some mahatmas. They live in the midst of wealth running into crores, he said."

Mother: "We cannot evaluate them on such grounds. Look at all the ornaments adorning the idols in temples. Do we blame God for all that? People do not think about all the good actions of mahatmas."

Venu: "He has some complaints about you too, Amma. He thinks that Amma ignores women."

Mother (laughing): "Oh, is that so?"

Venu: "Even though Amma is a woman, there are not too many brahmacharinis here, he complains."

Mother: "Would Amma, who wanted to do tapas to remove the weakness of women, now ignore women? For a life of sannyasa, one needs a good amount of manliness. Only girls with good masculine qualities should be accepted into ashrams. Otherwise, there will be only harm from them, even though they have come with the hope of helping the world. If boys err, the world won't blame so much. Even if they leave the ashram, they can find some work and earn a livelihood. But girls are not like that. They have to be very careful. And they need the ability to support themselves, even if they find out that they are not suited for ashram life. That is why Amma is insisting that all the girls here should continue their education. Girls have to be self-reliant. They are by nature compassionate. They form attachments easily. Because of this, they come to suffer. And they get cheated. But they will be saved, if their tendency to form bonds with everything is turned towards God. If a woman has the dispassion of a man, she will bring the benefit that ten men can."

Br. Pai: "Amma, which is more valuable, selfless action or meditation?"

Mother: "Children, what do you think?"

Each of them gave their opinion. It ended in a heated debate. Mother enjoyed it, listening with a smile on Her face. Finally everyone became quiet and looked at Her. "Amma, please tell us, yourself!" When their insistence became stronger, Amma said:

"You need both. Tapas alone is not enough, you need action also. Soap alone is not enough for washing the clothes; you need to agitate or beat the clothes clean. To overcome the circumstances, *karma* - action - is essential. We should be able to remember God constantly, whatever we are doing, not just when we sit for meditation. And selfless action will help bring the purity needed for meditation. Action is also necessary to test the progress we have made in meditation. On the other hand, without meditation, selfless action is not possible. The action of a man of *tapas* has a power of its own; it becomes beneficial to everyone."

Dr. Sudhamsu Chaturvedi, a college professor, arrived in the evening to see Mother. He was born in Uttar Pradesh in the north, but had been living in Kerala for many years. He spoke Malayalam fluently. He debated many topics with the brahmacharis in the ashram for a long time before Amma returned from Her trip. In his opinion, the most important thing was scriptural study.

Finally, Amma returned from Kollam. She sat down in the south-eastern corner of the kalari. Sudhamsu prostrated and sat down near Her. Without any introduction, Amma started to speak.

Mother: "Son, you travel frequently. When you are at the station, how do you know the schedule of the trains or buses?"

Sudhamsu: "I would ask at the counter or look at the schedule posted at the station."

Mother: "Having read the sign that tells you which bus goes where and when, will you stand there looking at the sign or will you find the bus and board it?"

Sudhamsu: "When I get the information, of course, I will get in the bus and travel. Only then I can reach my destination!"

Mother: "In the same way, the scriptures only point the way, son! If you just sit and read them, you will not reach your goal. When you wanted to come here, you found the appropriate bus and got into it. That is how you were able to reach here. Similarly, only by actually doing the sadhana described in the texts you achieve spiritual experience. By eating the picture of a banana, you will not get either the taste of banana or the benefit of eating it. Scriptural study is necessary, but you need sadhana also at the same time to get the benefit."

The professor was stunned by the fact that Amma knew exactly what he and the brahmacharis were discussing just before She came. He paused for a while and asked another question.

Sudhamsu: "If Christ was really a mahatma, couldn't he have prevented his opponents from crucifying him?"

Mother: "Christ was making that self-sacrifice to teach others the greatness of sacrifice and forgiveness. Mahatmas can remove their suffering in an instant, if they desire. But what they desire is to set an example for the whole world even if it means suffering on their part. No one can do anything to mahatmas. You can't even approach them without their consent. No one can oppose them, if they resolve against it. They willingly undergo suffering to teach the world how to face opposing forces and adverse circumstances."

Sudhamsu raised a different question: "How did all these brahmacharis arrive here as permanent residents?"

Mother: "Son, when a flower blossoms, there is no need to send out a special invitation to anyone to come and enjoy the honey. The bee will arrive on its own. These children had a spiritual *samskara* in them to begin with. Meeting Amma awakened it, that is all. Don't you recall the a forgotten song in its entirety when you hear the first line? These children were ready to lead a life in accordance with the samskara already in them. Amma is just guiding them, that is all."

Sudhamsu: "I have been practicing japa and meditation for a long time, but there is not enough progress."

Mother: "You have to have love for God, too. No amount of japa and meditation will bear fruit without love. When the love for God becomes firm, all the bad vasanas in us will drop away automatically. It is difficult to row a boat against the current. But if there is a sail, it becomes easy. The love for God is like a sail that helps the boat go forward.

"When two lovers are sitting together, they will be very

annoyed if some one else goes near them. A sadhak should have the same attitude. He wouldn't like anything that is not related to the Lord. He lives with the thought of God always in his mind. He wouldn't bear anything that becomes an obstacle to it. Compared to the love for God, everything else is worthless for him.

"Son, one should have true *lakshya bodha* (sense of one's goal). Only then, the sadhana one does will become deep. When some one sets out with a strong desire to reach some place, no obstacle will stop him. If he misses the bus, he will take a taxi. But if he is not truly interested, he will decide to go home if he misses the bus, thinking that he would try again the next day. Children, without intensity in sadhana, it is difficult to reach the goal.

"Before you sow the seed, you have to prepare the land, clearing it of grass and weeds. Otherwise it is difficult for the seeds to sprout. In the same way, we can enjoy the bliss of the Self, only if we turn the mind away from external things and direct it to God.

"Did you eat, son? Amma forgot that in the middle of the conversation."

"Yes, Amma."

The conversation turned to personal problems of the devotees. The hearts that were burning in the heat of samsara were cooled by the nectar of Mother's love.

Monday August 12, 1985

It was very late when the bhava darshan ended last night. Even after the darshan was over, Amma was immersed in talking with the devotees and offering consolation for their sorrows.

She tried especially hard to give solace to a woman devotee. She had been seeing Mother for a year. Her daughter was in the hospital with cancer. Many treatments were tried in vain. Thus she was in great distress mentally and physically and facing financial ruin when she heard about Amma from a friend and came to see Her. Amma gave Her some sacred ash to give her ailing daughter. Soon, the disease began to abate. The pain went away completely. More than that, a strength to face anything began to appear in the young woman. The doctors who had given the case up as hopeless were astonished by all this. She became well and didn't to have to stay in the hospital much longer. After coming home, both mother and daughter came to see Amma several times. During their last visit, Amma indicated that an operation would soon be needed. A week later, the daughter got worse and was readmitted to the hospital. The doctors recommended another operation. It was to take place in two days. The mother had come to get Amma's blessings before the operation. She was going back home early in the morning. Amma arranged for her to travel with a family of devotees from Trissur. As Amma was ready to go back to Her room, the crows had begun to caw announcing the arrival of another day.

Today the crowd of devotees is small. Mother reached the darshan hut at three in the afternoon. A brahmachari was meditating in the hut. Seeing that Amma had come in, he prostrated fully before Her. Taking the opportunity to talk to Amma before the devotees arrived, he submitted to Her a doubt that was bothering him:

"Amma, what is the relation between karma and rebirth? It is said that rebirth is caused by karma."

Mother: "Son, there is an aura around our bodies. Just as our words may be recorded on tape, all our actions leave their impression on this aura. The aura becomes golden if the actions are good. Whatever such people set out to do, the obstacles are eliminated and everything turns out auspiciously. The aura of those who do evil deeds becomes dark. Such people are never free of obstacles and problems. Their aura remains down here after their death, becoming food for worms and insects. Such people are destined to be reborn here."

When the devotees started arriving for darshan, the brahmachari prostrated and got up.

Mother began asking the devotees about their welfare. One devotee offered at Her feet a gift packet wrapped in brightly colored paper.

Mother: "*Mone*, how is your son doing?"

Devotee: "He got his job back because of your grace, Amma. There was a letter from his wife just the other day. He has stopped smoking ganja. He is well-behaved. He talks only about you. He sent his first salary to me. The letter specially asked me to give you all the news and get your blessings. That is why I came today."

Mother: "Amma is happy just to know that he has stopped smoking ganja. Son, tell him that Amma is pleased more by the change in his behavior than by the present he has sent."

The devotee's son worked in Bhilai. He had lost his job

when he started smoking ganja excessively and had to spent a year back home in Kerala without a job. It was during that time that he came to see Mother. Amma's heart melted seeing his sincere desire to free himself from his bad habit. She gave him some musk pills with Her blessing, and asked him to take a pill every time he had the urge to smoke ganja. He was able to reduce the smoking gradually and finally stop it completely. And he got his old job back unexpectedly just a couple of months ago.

The devotee continued: "All the pills Amma gave were used up before he left home. Now he keeps some musk in his pocket. He says just its smell is enough."

Mother: "That is because of his faith. Son, if there is faith, not only musk but even stones will give result."

Amma will not claim that anything happens due to Her powers. She who resides in the Supreme state, teaches through Her own action what total surrender to the Supreme means.

Saturday, August 24, 1985

Mother reached Kodungalloor yesterday. There was bhajan at the Devi temple in the evening. Every one spent the night at the home of a devotee. In the morning the brahmacharis performed Lalita Sahasranama archana and Amma did *arati* with camphor. After visiting the homes of three more devotees, they started the return trip to the ashram.

They stopped by the roadside for lunch. The family which hosted them last night had packed lunch for all. Every one sat in a circle. Amma served food on banana leaves. After reciting the fifteenth chapter of the Gita, they chanted *brahmarpanam* and ate their lunch. Someone got a container from a house near by and fetched water from the tap for everyone to wash hands. The people who watched this scene might have wondered who these nomads were and where they came from! Amma travels around the country with no thought of food or sleep, shedding the light of eternal peace in the path of Her children floundering in ignorance. When She comes running to comfort Her children who are deluded by *maya* and to give them everything She has, how can they know of Her own supreme sacrifice?

Clearing the doubts of the brahmacharis

They did not rest after lunch. The journey continued. Br. Venu had a severe ear ache that started the night before. He couldn't sleep at night. Amma made him sit near Her in the van. She asked others sitting nearby to move so that Venu could lie down. She put his head in Her lap and comforted him. "This ear ache came because you forcefully held your breath during pranayama," Amma said.

Venu: "Are you saying it is wrong to do pranayama?"

Mother: "No, it is not wrong. But you children don't have the patience to do it properly. In the old days, people were healthy and had patience. So they could practice these things properly. These days people have neither health nor patience. It is very dangerous to practice pranayama without the direct supervision of the guru."

Because of the crowd of devotees at the ashram, the brahmacharis often did not get time to talk to Mother about spiritual matters. Only during trips did everyone get a chance to sit near Her and listen to Her divine words.

A brahmachari: "Amma, who is greater, guru or God?"

Mother: "Guru and God are the same, in principle. But we may say that guru is above God. Guru's grace is something special. If the guru wants, he can remove the effect of God's displeasure. But even God cannot wipe away the sin arising from dishonoring the guru. When you realize God, you can say that you are the same as God. But even then you cannot say that you and the guru are the same. It is the guru who initiated the disciple to mantra that led to self-realization. It is the path shown by the guru that led the disciple to the goal. The guru will always have that special status. Even after realizing the truth, the disciple will stand in front of the guru with great humility."

Br: "Amma, how many times do we have to chant the mantra given by you to achieve *mantrasiddhi*?"

Mother: "What is important is not how many times you chant it, but how you chant it. How can you get any benefit from the mantra even if you chant it millions of times if, at the same time, you lead a heedless life, a life without *shraddha*? We can decide how many times a mantra should be chanted only by looking at how big or small it is. Japa should be done with one-pointedness. When japa is done with utmost concentration, the number of chanting is not important. Even a relatively small number will lead to *mantrasiddhi*. One must have concentration in the sound or form of the mantra. You can also focus on each letter of the mantra separately while chanting. You will not get one-pointedness always. That is why it is said that one should chant it some crores of times. The more you chant, the more one-pointedness you will get.

"Asking how many times one should chant the mantra is like asking how much water should be given to a plant for it to yield fruits. Watering is required, but the amount of water depends on the nature of the plant, the climate, the quality of the soil and so on. And water alone is not enough. The plant needs sunlight, fertilizer, air and protection from pests as well. Similarly, in the spiritual path, chanting the mantra is only one part. Good deeds, good thoughts, association with virtuous people *(satsang)* are all necessary. When all these are present, then one gets the benefit according to God's will."

Br: "Can one achieve *siddhis* through chanting of the mantra?"

Mother: "*Siddhis* depend on your *bhavana*. Japa can lead to siddhis. However, if one uses such siddhis indiscriminately, one will slip from the path that leads to the ultimate goal. Don't think that you can lead any kind of life once you have been initiated to a mantra. Amma is watching you! Suppose you are traveling by bus. You have bought a ticket. But when the inspector comes to check your ticket, you don't have it. You will be asked to get out of the bus. There is no leniency!

"Once you get self-realization, you have all the siddhis. Realization is beyond all siddhis. Once you have it, the whole world is in your hands. But instead of wanting it, if you ask the Lord for siddhis, it is like struggling to reach the royal court and asking for a couple of gooseberries when you finally come in front of the king."

Br: "How long will it take to get the vision of God?"

Mother: "We cannot predict when we will see God. It

dependence on the yearning of the seeker and the effort put forth. If we travel in an ordinary bus, we cannot be sure when we will reach our destination, since the bus stops at many points along the way. But an express bus stops only at a limited number of places and so we can predict the arrival time more or less accurately. Similarly, if we think of God without wasting even a moment, and move forward with total detachment, we can reach the goal in a short time. If there is no intensity in sadhana, it is not easy to say when we will reach there. The scriptures sometimes say that it doesn't take even an instant to attain God realization. But at other places, it is said that it is difficult to achieve realization even in a hundred births. The intensity of the sadhana and the *samskara* achieved in the previous births determine the time needed to reach the goal. And sadhana doesn't mean sitting somewhere with eyes closed. We need constant awareness of the goal and ceaseless effort. We need purity of heart, above all. Once we get purity of heart, it is easy to get God's grace."

Br: "Amma, does vision of God mean the same thing as God-realization?"

Mother: "Some people get certain visions during meditation. In meditation, there is a state that is neither sleep nor the waking state. It may be called the dream state of meditation. It is mostly in such a state that one gets visions of various divine forms. We cannot call them vision of God. We shouldn't be enamored by such visions, either. We should go forward."

Two brahmacharis sitting at the back of the bus were not listening to Mother. They were engaged in some argument about a passage in the upanishad they were studying at the time. Frequently they looked at Mother to see whether She was listening to them. Finally, She stopped what She was saying and turned to them.

Mother: "Children, don't waste your time trying to decide whether the fruit on the tree is fully ripe or it just looks ripe or whether it may be infested. Get up there and pick the fruit! Don't waste your time arguing about this and that. Chant your mantra constantly. If you want spiritual progress, you need to make constant effort. there is no short cut!"

Experiences that evoke wonder

Br. Venu's headache was gone by this time, either because of Mother's magic touch or because he was drinking in the nectar of Her words.

When the van reached Alleppy, it refused to move forward any further. Br. Ramakrishnan, who was driving, became worried, as he could not find any reason for this. He looked at Mother helplessly. She did not say anything, but got out of the bus with a smile and started walking. The brahmacharis walked with Her. Br. Ramakrishnan also followed Her, to ask Her advice about calling some one to repair the car or renting another vehicle if there was a delay. But Mother did not utter a word. Her devotee Shekhar lived close to the place where the car had stopped. She went directly to his house. The members of that family were overjoyed when they saw Amma. They had been hoping for some time that Amma would visit their home. They knew that She would be returning from Kodungalloor today and were praying eagerly for Amma to visit them on Her way. They were talking only about Her that day. Some one was expressing the doubt whether Amma would come without an invitation just as She walked in. They could not believe their eyes. They welcomed Her respectfully and led Her to the puja room. She did *arati* with camphor. She called each member of the family to Her and removed all their pains through the medicine of Her sweet words.

Amma did not spend much time there. As she stepped out of the house, Ramakrishnan was standing there, brooding in silence. As Mother walked forward without saying anything, Ramakrishnan told Her gently "Amma, the van has not been repaired yet." She got in the van and sat down, saying, "You try to start it again, son!" Ramakrishnan started the van and it moved forward without any problem. He looked back at Amma with a beaming face. She just smiled.

It was 7:30 PM when they reached the ashram after visiting the houses of two more devotees along the way. The evening bhajan was going on. Br. Anish[9], who was a student at the Chinmaya Mission in Bombay, was waiting to see Mother. This was his first visit here and his first darshan of Mother. Amma sat down in the courtyard between the Vedanta school and the kalari and talked to Anish for a while. The brahmacharis joined the bhajan in the kalari. Anish also went in finally and stood there enraptured by the bhajan, forgetting everything else, and to him, the song they were singing seemed to tell the story of his own life: *Akalatta kovilil...*

> *In a distant temple a wick was constantly burning,*
> *Guiding those who are groping in the dark.*
> *In this way, Mother was showing Her compassion.*

---

[9] Now Swami Amritagitananda.

One day when I was wandering along that path,
the Radiant One beckoned me with her hand;
She opened the sacred door
Took some holy ash
And rubbed it on my forehead.

She sang the songs of God,
And made a place for me to sleep
With Her own hands.
A novel kind off dream then came to me
declaring the truth:
Why do you weep?
Don't you know that you have reached
The sacred feet of the Lord?

I awoke with a sigh
And I clearly saw the Lotus Face
I saw it so clearly.

Thursday, September 5, 1985

The tireless Mother

A group of devotees arrived after midnight last night. They had started in the evening from Kollam. Their car had some problem along the way and it was very late by the time they got it repaired. They thought of returning home as it was so late, but proceeded to the ashram anyway, because of the insistence of one of the children. They did not expect to see Mother during the night at all. But She was standing alone in the coconut grove in front of the ashram as if expecting some one. They forgot all their problems the instant they saw Her. Mother sat down and talked to them till four o'clock.

Amma had a bath and came down again at five. A brahmachari who saw this, begged Her to take some rest, as She had not slept at all during the night. And tonight there would be *bhava darshan* and again She would miss sleep. Mother said, "One should not sleep when *archana* is going on. We are doing all this with some divine *samkalpa*. Everyone should be awake and do the archana. Sleeping at such a time will lead to mishaps. If Amma sleeps during archana today, you will all do the same thing tomorrow. There won't be any discipline in the ashram."

Br: "But, Amma, if you don't take some rest, will it not affect your health?"

Mother: "God will take care of all that. Amma has not come here to take care of this body. You follow the rules regularly; nothing will happen to Amma's health."

Knowing that further insistence was useless, the brahmachari withdrew. Mother went to the meditation room and joined the archana along with the brahmacharis. After the archana, She came to the coconut grove and sat down. Gayatri brought Her a cup of tea. She drank half of it and gave the cup to Gayatri.

Mother called Br. Sarvatma Chaitanya. He normally lived in France, working to spread Amma's teachings. He was here now to see Amma. Sarvatma came and prostrated and sat down next to Mother.

Sarvatma: "Amma, I knew you did not sleep at all last night. That is why I didn't come to see you. Tonight is bhava darshan, again. You should rest at least for a little while. I will come to see you after that."

Mother: "Son, don't you have to go back? You don't need to worry about Mother's comfort. She has no sleep most nights. Where is the time to sleep during the nights of bhava darshan? On other nights, Amma starts to read letters. And it will be very late when She is finished.

"Staying up all night has become a habit with Amma. This didn't start just recently - it was like this from Amma's childhood. She wouldn't sleep because of the grief of not having seen God yet. If She felt sleepy, She would inflict wounds on Her own body to stray awake! She would be busy with household chores throughout the day. By the time She finished cleaning the dishes at night, others would be fast asleep. Only then She got a little time to pray undisturbed. She would stay up all night crying out to the Lord.

"Night is the best time to pray. Nature is quiet. Nobody would disturb you. No one would know even if you go to the sea shore. You can sit there in solitude."

Sarvatma's eyes filled as he thought about Amma's sacrifice and intense tapas. Amma changed the subject and asked him: "Son, what did you say you wanted to ask Mother?" But he just sat there silently looking into Her eyes.

Explanation of mission work

Amma said to Bri. Gayatri standing nearby: "This son went to many places to give talks. At some places there were plenty of listeners, but at other locations there were very few. He began to worry when the crowd was small. He began to think that people were not coming because his speeches were not good. (Turning to Sarvatma) Son, why should you worry about how many people came to hear you? Aren't you doing what Amma asked you to do? Be careful about only one thing. You should show great humility in your words and deeds. We should get down to the level of the people and bring them up.

"Children are interested in playing. They won't even come inside to eat on time. It is the mother's job to feed her child on time. Shouting at him or spanking him won't work. She should call him with love. She should talk to him at his level. Only then he would come in to eat. In the same way, people may not take to spiritual ideas instantly. We have to make them interested. Every one appreciates being approached with humility. Every one yearns for love. We should approach each person at his level and bring him up."

Sarvatma: "Some people ask whether it is appropriate to form organizations in the name of mahatmas."

Mother: "Son, you may avoid an individual's name, but if you form a movement of some sort, it will have to have a name in the end. For instance, take some ideal in stead of an individual's name. Let it be the path of love, or the path of the atman - whatever it is, it has to have a label. Then there will be some followers, and it will become a group or an organization. It will be known as the organization standing for love or sacrifice. After a while, there will be the picture of the person who started it. And, in the end it will be known after an individual or a few individuals.

"We need some sort of instrument in order to broaden the human mind that is selfish. We have to tie the mind to some ideal. It is like putting a wild horse in a cage and taming it. Some people go to a *satguru* for this. The guru's name is a symbol for the ideals which he teaches through his own life. Others may adopt some other method. If you avoid the framework of an organization, it is hard to bring the teachings to the people. Why should we forego the great service of an organization just because of some minor defects? You may ask why there is a fence around a farm patch. But the fence clearly serves a purpose. Whatever you start, there will be some limitations. Do not worry about them, son! Try to see only the good in everything. Teach the people to do the same thing. It is said that if you give a swan a mixture of milk and water, it can drink just the milk from it. View everything with a broad mind. Take only what is good. Lead your life with the awareness of what is transient and what is eternal.

"One uses the first letter of the father's name as an initial in one's own name. Does the father gain anything from this? When we start an institution, countless people come there. They benefit from it. A sannyasin does not live for himself; he lives to teach others the supreme principle. The disciples spread the teachings of their guru just for this purpose. Ashrams are also for this.

"Do not see mahatmas as individuals. They stand for an ideal, for the ultimate principle. That is what we should look at. The guru is the principle of the Self that fills the whole universe. He may just appear to us as an individual. We should see as individuals only those who live for their families or to fulfill their own desires. Bur are mahatmas like that? They benefit the whole world. They bring peace to thousands of people.

"Son, most of us have grown up leaning on various individuals. Only a few people are able to grow up solely depending on the inner principles. In childhood, we depend on our parents. Later on, we lean on our friends or on our spouses. Thus we learn to love and serve only individuals. We are unable to live solely for principles. But mahatmas are beyond name and form even though they have names and forms. Even when you see them acting as individuals, there is no ego in them. There is no sense of the individual. If we lean on them, we can grow very fast and gain a breadth of vision."

Mother got up slowly. Sarvatma Chaitanya prostrated to Her. After giving a kiss to the son who was going away, Amma went to the hut to give darshan to the devotees.

There were some flower pots in the space between the darshan hut and the Vedanta school. Some of the plants were in bloom. Two brahmacharis were standing there enjoying the beauty of the flowers. Seeing Amma coming their way, they stepped aside. Seeing that one of the pots held a withering plant, She said to them: "One can see from this how alert you all are to external things. Would this plant have withered if you had *shraddha*? Didn't it dry up because no one watered it on time? One can find out how much *shraddha* a brahmachari has towards the world by just looking at the plants around him. One who loves God will love all living things and care for them as needed."

Mother went into the hut and started receiving devotees.

Unniyappam

A female devotee had brought some *unniyappam* (a sweet snack made of rice flour and brown sugar and fried in oil) for the brahmacharis. She offered them to Mother.

Mother: "Daughter, if you bring these children things like this, what is the use of their leaving home? They are here to practice renunciation. What will Amma do, if some one comes with food from the home of each brahmachari?"

Woman: "Amma, we bring these things only once in a while! What harm can it do?"

Mother: "To give them the things they crave is to hurt them, daughter. That is not showing them love. True love is not giving them food that pleases the palate. True love is inspiring them to control their palate and their mind, and helping them do that. When food passes down the throat, it turns into excreta. But one who controls the mind can always taste nectar. It is not possible to control the mind without controlling the palate. If these children craved for the pampering by their parents and for tasty food, what is the need of coming here? They have given up their home and surroundings and come here with a different goal in mind."

The woman's eyes filled with tears. "Amma, I didn't know that I committed such a grave error. I see every one here as my children. I don't think of anything but their welfare."

Amma pulled the woman close to Her and hugged her.

Mother: "Daughter, Amma wasn't trying to make you unhappy. She was just trying to know your mind. Some body here must have craved for *unniyappam*. That is why you brought it today!" (Mother laughs and every one in the hut joins Her.) "Even though Mother said these things, She sometimes makes tasty food for Her children here. She would think, 'How much comfort these children were accustomed to, at home! Will they be happy with the food here? Who else but Amma will make special treats for them now?' So, on some days Amma Herself makes special snacks for them. On some days, She would be thinking like this and some devotees would bring special things. The children here have not felt the lack of anything, by God's grace. But then, at times, Amma's attitude will change! She will give them just plain rice. There won't be anything to go with it. Sometimes, She will create circumstances in which the children will have to starve. After all, they have to be used to that as well. One shouldn't be the slave of the palate. Only if one foregoes the taste of the tongue can one enjoy the taste of the heart."

Amma called Bri. Gayatri and entrusted her with the unniyappam to give to the ashram inmates. Gayatri had not heard the conversation that took place in the hut. She took the packet from Amma and whispered something in Her ear. Amma started laughing loudly. Every one looked at Her face wondering what was going on.

Mother: "Didn't Amma say that someone must have craved for unniyappam? Apparently, one son told Gayatri about the times he had eaten it at home and said how nice it would be to taste it again.!" (Everybody laughs.)

The darshan lasted till two in the afternoon. Before returning to Her room, Amma went to the dining hall and made sure that all the people were being fed well. It was a night of bhava darshan. Amma would come down again at five o'clock for bhajan, which would start early since it was a day of *bhava darshan*.

Friday, September 6, 1985

Br. Neal Rosner[10] was busy recording the daily activities of the ashram on video tape. He was using a video camera brought by a devotee from the US the day before. He had already recorded the Veda chanting and Sahasranama archana that took place early in the morning. But the recording was not very good, probably because Amma did not allow the use of any additional lighting.

"If you turn on bright lights during archana, every one will lose concentration," Amma told Nealu. "The mind should be focused fully on the chosen deity or on the mantra. The Divine Mother is present where we do the archana. The purpose of archana is to focus our minds. We should understand that."

Mother often says that spiritual, seekers should not allow their pictures to be taken. 'The flash light robs the seeker of his powers,' She would say. Mother constantly reminds us to concentrate totally on whatever we are doing.

Mother did not allow the video recording initially. Nealu followed Her around all of last night. "Amma, we get letters daily from abroad, asking for a video picture of you. There are so many of your children abroad, who are unable to come here. Isn't this for them? They sent this camera, in fact. Please, just this one time, Amma..." Finally Amma agreed to Nealu's entreaties. "All right, if you insist. But don't obstruct the children's meditation or anything. Also, don't stand in front of me holding that thing!" Nealu had to agree to these conditions.

Nealu stood behind a coconut tree, waiting for Mother to come to the darshan hut. There was not enough light because

---

[10] Now Swami Paramatmananda

of the trees. And Amma wouldn't allow extra lighting for picture taking. Amma finally came. She walked to the hut, brightening up the shaded areas under the coconut trees. And Nealu followed Her enjoying the scene through the camera's eye.

The renunciate and relatives

The biological mother of one of the brahmacharis was waiting to see Amma. Her daughter was also with her. The woman bowed to Amma and explained the reason for her sadness.

Woman (pointing to the brahmachari): "Amma, we are celebrating his father's birthday. Please let him come home for a couple of days!"

Mother: "But Amma has not forbidden any one from going out of the ashram, daughter! You can, of course, take him with you if he likes to go."

Woman: "He is not agreeing. He will obey only your words, Amma!"

The brahmachari was standing there with lowered head. His mother and sister were pleading to Amma!

Amma turned to him. "Why son, can't you go with them?" He nodded halfheartedly. All three bowed to Her and went out of the darshan hut.

In the afternoon, as Amma came out after the last of the devotees had left, She was greeted by the hapless face of the brahmachari.

Mother: "You didn't go? Where are your mother and sister?"

Br: "They left. I somehow sent them away."

Mother: "Didn't you want to be home for your father's birthday feast?"

Br: "No, Amma. I will be happy if you don't press me to go! My only sadness is that I didn't obey your words!"

Amma was on the way to Her room. She stopped. She was not smiling. On Her face, there was a seriousness filled with love. Amma sat down on the steps. The brahmachari sat at Her feet. Amma looked straight into his eyes.

Mother: "Son, a seeker should not maintain his relation to his family. That is like rowing a boat which is tied to a tree. He will not progress in his sadhana. It is the same way if your mind is filled with thoughts. It is like rowing a boat in waters overgrown with seaweed. You may row a hundred times, but you would move only an inch!

"When you talk to your family members or read their letters, you are exposed to all the news about home and the neighborhood. Then, what meaning is there in saying that you have left home? Your mind will hover around your home and neighborhood. With all those thoughts, how can you get any concentration? There will only be waves of thoughts. Seekers shouldn't read even the newspaper in the beginning. When you read the paper, all the news of the world will leave their imprint on your mind. Some children read the newspaper, and come and tell Amma all the stories. Amma will pretend to be hearing everything, to take a measure of their own minds. The next day they come again with more stories. You children don't know that this is not what Amma expects from you! A brahmachari should have the attitude of total surrender to the Lord. He should have the conviction that the Lord will take care of his family. If there is that firm faith, God will, indeed, take good care of the family members. Didn't Krishna himself come to the aid of Kuroor Amma?[11]

"Son, if we pour water at the root of a tree, it will reach all the branches. But if we pour it on the branches, the tree does not benefit. And our effort is wasted. If we love God, it is equal to loving every one. It benefits every one. The same Lord dwells inside every one. Through loving Him, we love all. But if we form bonds only to individuals, it will just lead to sorrow.

"When we start learning to drive, we should go to an empty lot and practice. Otherwise, we may be a danger to ourselves and to others. But once we have learnt to drive well, we can handle the car easily even in heavy traffic. Likewise, a sadhak should stay away from family and friends in the beginning, and practice solitude. Otherwise, it will be difficult to tie the mind to God. But, as he progresses in his sadhana, he will be able to see everybody as the Lord, and love and serve them. His spiritual strength will not be wasted. But, son, if you keep up your relation to the family now, you will lose whatever strength you have. So it is enough to write a letter to your mother now. Write only about spiritual matters. If you happen to go home, sleep only in the puja room. If someone comes to tell you family matters, don't lend your ears. Talk only about spiritual things."

Amma's words consoled the brahmachari. He prostrated and left. Amma went to Her room.

---

[11] Kuroor Amma was a brahmin lady who was a great devotee of Lord Krishna as manifested in the temple at Guruvayur. There are many stories in which Krishna came to her aid in times of need.

On the seashore

It was five-thirty in the evening. Mother came down from Her room and called all the brahmacharis to the sea shore. When they reached the beach, She was already in deep meditation. Every one sat around Her. There was only the sound of the sea.

Mother opened Her eyes after two hours. She got up and started walking slowly on the beach. As darkness descended slowly, Amma's white clothes took on an even greater glow. The waves were competing to kiss Her feet. The four or five waves which got that rare chance calmly dissolved back into the ocean with contentment.

Mother began to sing softly as She continued to walk along the seashore absorbed in a divine mood, with eyes fixed on the horizon. Those who followed Her sang along.

Omkaramengum

The sound 'Om' resonates everywhere
Echoing in every atom
With a peaceful mind
Let us chant 'Om Shakti.'

The tears of sadness are overflowing
and now Mother is my only support.
Bless me with Your beautiful hands
For I have given up all worldly enjoyments.

The fear of death has disappeared:
The desire for physical beauty is gone.
I must constantly remember your form

That shines with the light of Shiva.

When I am filled with an inner light
That overflows and shines before me,
and I am drunk with devotion,
I will merge in the beauty of Thy form.

Your form is what I have longed to see the most.
All existing loveliness has crystallized
And comes as this unequaled Beauty.
Oh, now my tears are overflowing...

When the song ended, Mother walked back to the ashram. No one spoke. When they reached the ashram, the bhajan was over. Mother sat down in the sand on the western side of the ashram. Seeing that She wanted complete solitude, the others withdrew, one by one.

Instructions to the brahmacharis

Mother emerged after giving darshan to the devotees, and walked towards the brahmacharins' huts. She would inspect the rooms of the brahmacharis occasionally. She would check to see if everything in the rooms were arranged neatly, if there were things kept for private use that were not really essential, and if the rooms were being swept daily. It was impossible to fool Amma. She didn't even like to see more than one library book in any room. There shouldn't be even one more dhoti or shirt than absolutely necessary. One day, noticing that a brahmachari had a grass mat spread over a piece of carpet to sleep on, Amma remarked, "We used to sleep on the floor. It would be a bare cement floor or a floor covered with cow dung. There won't be any spread or cover, usually. Sometimes, the whole family would sleep together on mats spread on the floor, and little babies would wet the mats. That is how we grew up. Even now, Gayatri will tell you that Amma sleeps mostly on the bare floor, even though She has a cot and a mattress. You children grew up in comfort at home. It would be hard for you to sleep on the dirt floor." The brahmachari quickly rolled up the carpet.

Today, Amma went inside one of the huts and picked up a packet from under the writing table. She seemed to know exactly where it was, as if She had kept it there Herself.

"What is this, son?," She asked the brahmachari who lived in the hut. His face went pale. Mother opened the packet. It contained *ariyundas* (sweet balls made from rice flour).

"Your parents brought these for their darling son, right?" The brahmachari lowered his head. That was true. His parents had brought them the day before. He had asked them to give the packet to Bri. Gayatri, to distribute to every one. But they wouldn't listen. "We brought a separate packet for Amma and Her other children. This is just for you," they said. When they insisted, he didn't object.

Some other brahmacharis had followed Mother into the hut. She gave each one an *ariyunda*.

Mother: "Son, Amma would like to see you slice even a banana into a hundred pieces and give every one a piece. Lot of people bring sweets and snacks for Amma. But She can't eat anything by Herself. She would keep everything for Her children. Sometimes, She would put a pinch of something in Her mouth, just to please them. Do you know how much trouble some people go through to make something for Amma, to pack it and bring it here, spending money on bus fare and other things?

"Son, did Amma make you unhappy?"

Mother put the brahmachari on Her lap. She broke one of the sweets and after putting a bit in Her own mouth, fed him the rest. This only increased his sorrow. Amma said, "Don't cry, my son! Amma is saying these things only so that you don't keep your attachment to the family. At least you didn't eat all of this yourself, but kept some aside. If it were some one else, we wouldn't have seen even the paper it was wrapped in, right?" She asked the others with a smile.

To change the subject, Mother reached over and picked up a book. The book was covered with dust. She tapped the dust off. It was a primer on Sanskrit.

Mother: "Haven't you been going to the Sanskrit class?"

Br: "I didn't go to the last two or three classes, Amma! The grammar doesn't stick to my mind at all."

Mother: "Looking at this book, it seems that you haven't touched it for at least a month. You shouldn't show this kind of negligence towards your text books, son. Learning is a form of Devi Sarasvati. You should approach learning with shraddha and devotion. Whenever you pick up or put down a book, you should touch it with reverence and bow to it. Keep the books neat. That is what we all learnt.

"If you are reluctant to learn Sanskrit, how will you understand our scriptures? Sanskrit is our mother. You can't fully appreciate the upanishads or the Gita without Sanskrit. To understand the mantras and the chants, you should learn them in that language. It is the language of our culture. We can't separate the culture of India from Sanskrit. It is true that we can buy the translations of the scriptural texts in other languages, but they don't amount to the real thing. If you want to know the taste of honey, you should taste it by itself. If you mix it with something else, you won't get its true taste. Even uttering Sanskrit words is good for the health of our minds.

"But you should understand one thing, children. You shouldn't be learning Sanskrit just to show off your knowledge. It should be only to enhance your mental refinement. You should view Sanskrit only as an instrument for that. Once you find out from the newspaper ads where you can get mangos, the smart thing is to buy them and enjoy them, not just staring at their picture in the paper. Anyway, don't worry, son! Try to learn Sanskrit diligently at least from now on!"

Someone brought up the name of a Sanskrit scholar who had come to the ashram recently. The conversation continued on the subject of learning Sanskrit.

Mother: "Son, it is good to know Sanskrit. But we don't need to spend a lifetime learning grammar. If you go out in front of people today just displaying your knowledge of Sanskrit, they won't appreciate it much. All the scriptures emerged from the minds of the sages who led a life of *tapas*. Tapas makes everything clear and transparent. A person who does tapas can learn in a day what an ordinary person learns in ten days. Therefore, tapas is the important thing. Sanskrit and Vedanta are important; one should learn them. But we learn things to know what our life's goal is and what path would lead us to it. Once we know that, we should try to advance on that path.

"When we get to a railway station, we should look up the train schedule, buy the ticket and get on the appropriate train.

Many people who consider themselves scholars are like those who stay at the station memorizing the train schedule. They don't put their learning to use.

"Take a big bag of sugar. Do we have to eat all of it to know that it is sweet? When we are hungry, we should eat just enough food to appease our hunger. We don't have to eat everything in the kitchen. The so-called scholars don't think that way. They seem to want to eat the whole thing. And they waste their lives that way. If you look at most of the scholars of today, you will see that they have only learning, no experience. And what is the result? Even after learning till the age of ninety, there is no freedom from sorrow. Most of them sit at home, recalling what they have learnt. If they had learnt what is needed and at the same time done tapas, that knowledge would have done them and the world some good. That is why Amma says that you should learn the scriptures up to a point, but then you should do tapas. Only that would bring your learning to the plane of experience, bring peace to you and enable you to do some thing good for the world.

"After you have learnt enough and gained some strength through spiritual discipline, you should serve others. That would save a lot people. There are some individuals who sit in front of the temple reading the Gita and the upanishads, but would shrink from any one approaching them, saying 'Don't touch me, don't touch me!' What kind of devotion do they have? A tape recorder will repeat what others have already said. Similarly, these people just spit out the words of wisdom someone else has said before. But they can't put those to work in their own lives. They can't show love to anyone. They are never free of pride and jealousy. What is the use of such scholarship? Children, you should have love for your fellow beings and compassion towards those who suffer. Without that we can never reach God. We would just be selfish beings."

A brahmachari who was listening to Mother asked, "If meditation will lead to true knowledge, why can't we just meditate all the time? What are classes for? What is *karmayoga* for?"

Mother: "That is fine. But who can meditate every hour of the day? Do we get concentration even for five minutes if we sit for an hour? That is why Amma says that we have to work for the benefit of the world, after we set apart some time for meditation. One shouldn't doze off in the name of meditation and become a burden to the world. We happen to be born; now we have to do some good for the world before we depart. Of course, if there is someone who can meditate twenty-four hours a day, that is great. Amma will not send them anywhere. She will give them all the facilities they need. But once they sit for meditation, they should truly meditate. It is not meditation, if the mind is roaming around in a thousand other places while you sit in one spot. The mind has to be fixed on God. Then it becomes meditation. If you do your work, remembering God and chanting your mantra, that is also meditation. Meditation is not only just sitting still.

Br: "What service are you suggesting we should do for the world, Amma?"

Mother: "Son, today people are lost without knowing what culture means. We should make them understand what real samskara is. Countless people are suffering from poverty - both material and spiritual poverty. We should try to eliminate that. If we don't have any food to give to those who are hungry, we should even go out and beg for food to feed them. That is what real strength means. We should not be doing tapas just for our liberation; it should be to gain strength to serve the world. When we get a compassionate mind like that, God realization will follow very soon. We can get to our goal faster than by tapas alone. (Laughing) But what good is someone who sits around, half asleep, in the name of tapas, serving no one at all?"

Br: "Let us learn who we are first, Mother. Can't we wait till then to start serving the world? Right now, so many people are claiming to be serving the world. The world has not changed a bit. On the other hand, isn't it true that just one individual who has attained liberation can change the whole world?"

Mother closed Her eyes. She remained looking inward for a little while. Then She opened Her eyes slowly.

Mother: "Children, if you say that you can't do service, that you just want liberation, then show that kind of intensity! Those who have that kind of yearning will not let even a moment pass without remembering God. Eating and sleeping will mean nothing to them. Their hearts will be aching for God always."

Memories of Mother's childhood

Mother seemed to be recalling the very touching scenes of Her childhood and Her eyes became full of tears.

Mother: "Once Amma started searching for God, She was writhing in agony till She reached the goal. The tears never stopped. There was no sleep. When the sun set, the heart was violently agitated. Wasn't another day lost? Didn't She waste another day without knowing the Lord? That sorrow was too much to bear. She would stay awake all night, thinking that if She didn't sleep, the day would not be lost. Always, there was the quest, 'Where are you? Where are you?' Unable to bear the sorrow of not seeing the Lord, She would bite and tear up Her own body. Sometimes She would roll around on the floor, crying out aloud, calling the Lord's names. She would burst into tears spontaneously. She wouldn't feel like laughing at all. What good is your laughter when you haven't yet known God? 'Why should I rejoice without knowing you? Why should I eat when I don't know you? Why bathe?' Amma got through each day in this manner."

Mother stopped for a moment and then continued: "When you get severe detachment, you may dislike the world. But you have to get beyond that stage also. You have to see that everything is God.

"Amma felt great love towards poor people when She was young. When they starved, She would steal food from home and bring it to them. Later, when She was in grief as She hadn't yet seen God, She turned against the whole world. She felt angry at Nature. She would say, 'I don't like you at all, Mother Nature, since you make us do wrong things!' She would spit at Mother Nature and shout at her using whatever words that came to Her mouth. It became a form of madness. When food was placed in front of Her, She would spit into it. It was a very difficult condition. She would be angry at everything. She felt like throwing mud at anyone who came near. When She saw someone suffering, She would think that it was their selfishness and that they were just experiencing the fruits of their karma. But this attitude also changed soon. She started thinking, 'People are making mistakes out of ignorance;

only if we forgive them and love them, they will stop making mistakes. If we get angry at them, won't they just repeat their bad actions?' When these thoughts came, Her heart was filled with compassion. Her anger disappeared completely."

Amma sat immersed in meditation for a little while. Everyone drew mental pictures of Amma's childhood according to their own imagination. Mother Nature who had witnessed those incomparable scenes was also very still. Amma said in a deep voice:

"Children, your heart should throb and ache for God constantly. There shouldn't be a single instant without remembrance of God. Only such people have attained salvation."

Amma's words of counsel on detachment and yearning for liberation touched the hearts of the listeners. They all stood there forgetting the external world.

CHAPTER FOUR

Friday, 20 September 1985

Brahmacharis and householders

Some devotees were standing in front of the meditation room. Mother came out after giving instructions on meditation to the brahmacharis. "Where are you from, children?," She asked the devotees.

Devotee: "From Kollam, Amma."

Mother: "Have you come here before, son?"

Devotee: "I set out two or three times to come here. But each time, I couldn't make the trip due to some unexpected reason. After all, isn't it true that our decision alone is not enough, for getting the darshan of mahatmas? I go to Kanyakumari often, on business, but so far I haven't been able to go and see Mayiamma there. I don't know why. I visit a lot of ashrams. Last year we went to Rishikesh as a family."

Mother: "You are finding time to do these things in the midst of your busy work. That itself is God's blessing."

Devotee: "This is the only thing that keeps me steady, Amma. Otherwise, how will I sleep peacefully in the middle of all the business activities? The relationship with ashrams and sannyasins are the wayside supports on which I unload life's problems to rest. If not for them, my life would have been confined to the liquor shop, long ago."

Mother: "O Shiva, Shiva!"

Devotee: "Amma, although I have visited many ashrams, I have not seen an atmosphere so full of divine essence as here. Also, I have not seen so many young inmates, anywhere else.

Mother: "The children who are here first saw Amma when they were in college or working at jobs. They threw away everything and came to Amma. Most of them did not know the meaning of spirituality or of meditation. They all seemed to get some form of madness when they saw Amma. Their mind was no longer on the job. Or on their studies. No one ate on time. No one washed clothes. They didn't pay attention to anything. They would never leave Amma's side. She tried to drive them off. But none of them would go. Finally, Amma had to accept defeat. She had to keep every one here. Even though Amma is everything to them, they still need to do sadhana. Today, they are not interested in anything external because of their love for Her. But they cannot maintain that without doing sadhana.

"Doesn't Amma have to look after, in every way, these children who have taken refuge in Her? In the past, She had time to take care of them. But now She is not able to give them enough attention, because of the increasing number of devotees. Therefore, whenever She gets time, She makes them sit down and meditate as She did just now. And She has told them to tell Her immediately when they have a problem. They don't have to wait for an appropriate time or anything. She is, after all, the only mother, father and guru they have!"

Devotee: "Amma, I am regretting that I am a householder. Will I be able to get self-realization?"

Mother: "Son, there is no householder or brahmachari in the eyes of God. He looks only at your mind. You can lead a truly spiritual life while remaining a householder. You will be able to enjoy the bliss of the Self. But your mind has to be in God all the time. Then you can attain bliss easily. A mother bird will be thinking of the young one in the nest, even when she is out looking for food. Similarly, you have to keep your mind on God, when you are engaged in all the worldly actions. The important thing is to have dedication to God or Guru. One you get that, your goal is not very far.

"Once, a Guru came with his disciples to a village to give spiritual discourses. A businessman came with his family everyday to hear the talks. By the time the satsangs were over, he became a devotee of the Guru. He and his family decided to live in the Guru's ashram.

"When the Guru returned to his ashram, he saw the businessman and family waiting for him. They told the Guru of their decision to live in the ashram. The Guru explained to them the difficulties of ashram life. But his explanations could not turn the devotee away. The Guru agreed in the end. The businessman and his family became permanent residents of the ashram.

"They took part in the ashram work just as the other inmates. But the other disciples did not like a householder living in the ashram with his family. They began complaining about the businessman and his family. The Guru decided to demonstrate to his disciples the strength of the new devotee's dedication. He called the devotee and said, 'You have given up your home and your wealth. You don't have anything. There are not enough resources here in the ashram, either. We somehow manage here because the brahmacharis work hard everyday. It would have been easy if you were single. It is hard to bear the expenses of your wife and children also. So from tomorrow onwards, you should go out and work and earn enough for their upkeep.' The devotee agreed gladly.

"The next day, he started to work in the town nearby and brought his earnings to the Guru in the evenings. After a few days the disciples began to complain again. So the Guru called the devotee again and said, 'The money you bring is enough for your expenses. But it is not at all enough for the upkeep of your wife and children. Since the ashram met all their expenses till now, you should work twice as much and pay off that debt to the ashram. Only after that you and your family should eat at the ashram.'

"The devotee called his wife and children and explained, 'Until we pay off the debt, we should not eat anything here. It would be a sin. It will be a burden to our Guru. I will bring you some food at night. You should wait patiently till then.' They agreed. From the next day onwards, he worked from morning till very late at night and gave all his wages to the Guru. He shared with his wife and children any food he got at the work place. Some days there was nothing, and everyone starved.

"The other disciples were astonished to see that the devotee and family didn't leave the ashram, in spite of all these difficulties. They complained again to the Guru, 'Nowadays, the businessman is coming back only late at night. He is making money working outside while his wife and children live comfortably here at the ashram. What a convenient arrangement!'

That night the Guru waited for the devotee. When he came and prostrated at his feet, the Guru told him, 'You are a cheat! Don't prostrate to me. You keep your family here, and you amass private wealth by working outside. But you claim that you are giving to the ashram everything you earn.' The devotee didn't say anything in reply. He listened to the Guru with folded hands. Then he silently went to his room.

"That night, the Guru called all the disciples and said, 'Tomorrow there will be a feast at the ashram. There is no firewood here. Someone should go to the forest now itself and bring firewood. We need it before sunrise.' He then went to bed. Who would go to the forest at such a late hour? The disciples awakened the devotee. They told him of the Guru's command to get firewood immediately for the feast next day. The devotee set out to the forest very gladly. The other disciples went to bed happily.

"When he didn't see the devotee at dawn the next day, the Guru called the other disciples and enquired about him. They replied that he had gone to gather firewood. The Guru went to the forest along with the disciples in search of the devotee. They searched everywhere, but couldn't find him. Finally, when they called out his name, they heard a voice in reply. The voice came from a large well. The devotee had slipped and fallen into the well while returning with firewood in the darkness. Although it was not very deep, it was difficult to climb out of the well without help. Also, since he had no food for several days before that, the poor man didn't have the strength to get out, carrying the firewood.

"It was very dark. The Guru asked the disciples to get the devotee out of the well. When they extended their hands into the well, they could feel a bundle of firewood. When they asked the devotee to raise his hands, he replied, 'If I let go, the firewood will fall into the water. I am holding it up so that it does not get wet. You should give this to our Guru as soon as possible. It is for the morning feast. It is enough to get me out after that.'

"The Guru's eyes filled with tears when he saw the dedication of his devotee. He asked the disciples to lift him out of the well immediately. But he agreed to come up only after someone took the firewood from him. The Guru embraced the devotee who was shivering with cold after being in the well for so long. He was so pleased with that selfless love and surrender that he blessed the devotee with self-realization immediately. Children, nobody loses the chance for self-realization because he is a *grihasthashrami*. Whether one is a brahmachari or a householder, the important thing is an attitude of faith and surrender to the guru."

A few moments with the brahmacharis

Br. Ramakrishnan brought some water for Amma to drink. From the way his lips moved, one could see that Ramakrishnan was always chanting his mantra.

Mother is very particular that one chants the mantra constantly when cooking and serving food for Her. One day Bri. Gayatri brought Her some tea. Amma gave the cup of tea back to Gayatri and said, "While you made this tea, your mind was not in what you were doing or in your mantra. You were thinking of Australia. You can drink this, yourself!"

Gayatri went back silently, remembering that she was talking to a brahmacharini about her early days in Australia while she was making the tea. She again made tea, this time with shraddha and constant chanting of her mantra. While drinking it, Amma said, "Your heart is in this. That is what prompts me to drink it more than the taste of it!"

Br. Ramakrishnan prostrated before Amma and sat near Her. The previous day, someone on the ferry had talked ill of the ashram. Ramakrishnan happened to hear it and he couldn't bear it. He reacted to them loudly. When he mentioned this incident, Amma said:

"Son, you were happy when every one praised Amma and showed love for all of you. You were satisfied when others nodded their heads in assent at whatever you said. You drank all that in like nectar. Where thousands of people gather, two or three of them may say things against you. That is when we should look inside us. We should see how patiently we can welcome such a situation. We shouldn't get angry at them. If we get angry at them and ask them not to come here again, do they get any benefit from our lives?

"Each one of or acts should benefit the world. It is when those students, who normally don't learn at all, are successful in the examinations that we truly appreciate the teacher's ability. We can claim that our life has been beneficial only if we can cultivate and reap a harvest from a land which lay neglected, covered with rubbish and weeds.

"The people you encountered just travel over the surface of the ocean. All they want is fish. We can't just go like that. We are looking for pearls. Only if we dive deep and search carefully, we may get even one of them. They may have said some things out of ignorance. But if we react to them angrily, who is really more ignorant? If we make a lot of noise, just like them, what will be the opinion of others about us? We should take care to maintain our balance even when others oppose us or talk ill of us. That is a sadhana. We should see that as an opportunity to measure the patience in us. We should welcome such situations with equanimity."

A brahmachari mentioned the case of three inmates of an ashram in north India who had come here recently and wanted to live here.

Mother: "Someone who visited their ashram had given them a copy of Amma's biography. When they read it, they immediately wanted to be near Her. They made up some excuse to leave their ashram and travel down here. Amma had to try hard to send them back. We shouldn't keep here those who come from other ashrams without the permission of the authorities there."

A group of devotees had gathered around Mother by this time. She took all of them to the darshan hut.

Feeding Her children

Mother talks often about the importance of vows and observances and in the life of a spiritual seeker. But She is against anyone becoming the slave of any particular vow or observance. Vows are a means of conquering the mind, not to become its slave. Special importance is given to fasting and the vow of silence. Mother has asked ashram inmates to fast and, if possible, observe silence every Saturday. This was being followed regularly. Some inmates observed silence throughout the day. They would talk only to Mother. Some of them maintained silence till six in the evening. Everyone was expected to remain in the meditation room till dusk. No one was expected to go out.

CHAPTER 4

On one Saturday, Amma put everyone in the meditation room at seven in the morning and locked the door from the outside. She had told them earlier that She expected them to spend the whole day in japa and meditation. They all took their seats and were soon immersed in meditation. They opened their eyes at nine o'clock hearing Amma's voice.

"Children..!"

There was a glass of sweet coffee in front of each of them. And some sweetened *aval* (a form of flattened rice) and two bananas. Mother was standing there with a smile.

"Children, you need to meditate only after eating this."

She closed the door and went out. They all ate Mother's prasad with devotion and then resumed their japa and meditation.

It was twelve-thirty. They heard a bell and looked at each other with astonishment. It was the lunch bell! The brahmachari who cooked lunch daily was in the meditation room. 'Who might have cooked lunch today? What is this new leela of Amma?' While everyone was wondering thus, a devotee came to inform them that Amma was calling them for lunch. They saw Mother waiting for Her children in the dining room. She had arranged their plates in the usual places, served rice and curries, and placed a glass of drinking water next to each plate. All they had to do was to eat. There was one more curry than usual. Amma's special! She Herself served them as they ate.

Mother told the householder devotees who were eating with the brahmacharis: "As Amma came out after putting the children in the meditation room, She began to think how cruel She was to make Her children starve like this! She went to the kitchen and saw that there was no food there. She prepared some sweet *aval* and some coffee. She found some bananas also. She put everything in front of the children. After all, only if they get out of the room their minds would wander. Also, She wanted to teach them the lesson that if we take refuge in God completely, He will bring everything we need right in front of us. Then She came back to the kitchen and cooked rice and vegetables. Since Amma had told the children that no one should be found outside, all of them remained in the meditation room. It has been a long time since Amma cooked something for Her children. At last, She was able to do that today. Amma is ready to starve for any length of time, but She doesn't have the strength to see Her children starving. With more and more devotees coming, Amma does not get as much time as before to pay attention to the children living in the ashram. She knows that God makes sure that they lack nothing."

A brahmachari had stopped on his way to the meditation room. He heard footsteps behind him and looked back. Mother was coming towards him with a smile on Her face. Br. Rao[12] was also with Her.

"What were you thinking about?" Mother asked.

"I happened to remember how you made us fast on a Saturday sometime ago."

Mother: "How come you remember it today?"

Br: "It is a Saturday today, isn't it?"

Mother: "Don't waste time standing here. It is time for meditation." She proceeded to the meditation room with them.

Mother told the brahmacharis waiting in the meditation

---

[12] Now Swami Amritatmananda.

room: "Children, don't try to arrest your mind by force when you sit down for meditation. The thoughts will rise up with ten times their original force if you do that. It is like pressing a spring down. Try to find out where the thoughts arise from and to control them with that knowledge. Don't put the mind in any kind of tension. If any part of your body is not relaxed or has any pain, the mind will linger over that. Relax every part of the body. And watch your thoughts with full awareness. Then the mind will subside by itself.

"Don't follow your thoughts. If you follow them, only your body will be here. Your mind will be somewhere else! Haven't you seen cars moving on a dusty road? They will stir up all the dust on the way. We won't be able to see the cars at all. If you are following such a car, we will just be bathed in dust. Even if we stand on the road side, we will be covered with dust. So when we see a car coming, we have to stand at a distance. In the same way, we should watch our thoughts from a distance. If we go near them, they will drag us also along without our knowledge. But if we watch from a distance, we can see the dust settling and peace returning."

Amma with Ottoor

Ottoor Unni Namboodiripad, a great devotee of Krishna and a celebrated poet, had come to live in the ashram. He was eighty-two years old and in very poor health. His wish was to die in Mother's lap. He was given a room built over the meditation cave, just behind the kalari.

It was nine at night. Mother went to Ottoor's room. There were some brahmacharis also in the room. Even though

Mother tried to stop him, Ottoor got down on the floor with great difficulty and prostrated to her. She helped him get up and made him sit on his bed and sat next to him. If She remained standing, he would not sit on the bed.

Ottoor: "Amma, please say something! Let me hear your words!"

Mother: "But you know everything, son!"

Ottoor: "Hasn't this son put all the brahmacharis into trouble?"

A brahmachari: "No, not at all! It is our good fortune that we got the opportunity to serve you. Where else would we get such good *satsang*?"

Mother: "Your first prayer should, indeed, be for the good fortune to serve the Lord's devotees. That is the only way for us to reach Him."

Seva and sadhana

Br: "But, Amma, isn't it true that service, however great it is, amounts only to karma yoga? But Sankaracharya has said that one attains self-realization only through *jnana*, even if the mind is purified through karma yoga."

Mother: "Son, the Self is not just confined within you, but pervades everything in this universe. We rise to the level of Self-realization only when we see that everything is the same. We won't be admitted to God's world without the signature of even the smallest ant on our entry papers. The first requirement, along with remembrance of God, is love for all living and nonliving things. If we have that greatness of heart, liberation won't be far behind.

"We go to the temple, circumambulate three times and bow down to the deity. On our way out, we kick the beggar who is at the door! That is our samskara now. We will fully deserve realization only when we see, even in that beggar, the One to whom we just prostrated. When working in the world, we should serve man, seeing him as God. Only then we will achieve humility and politeness. It is all over when one begins to feel, 'I am doing service to the world!' Anything we do with that attitude is not seva. Real seva means our words, smile and action accompanied by love and an attitude that 'I am nothing.'

"People don't know their real essence. Look at the little birds living near the pond. They don't know that they have wings. They don't want to fly high and enjoy the honey from the flowers on the trees around the pond. They just live on the dirt in the pond. But once they soar high and taste the honey, they will not go back to the dirt below. Similarly, people spend their lives ignorant of the bliss one gets from pure love of God. Our aim is to make them aware of that and to lead them to their true essence. That is your duty towards the ashram."

Br: "How can we perform selfless service without knowing the truth of the Self?"

Mother: "Children, service is also a form of sadhana. If you claim that you have become complete after doing sadhana sitting at a place, Mother will not accept that. Getting out into the world and doing service is very much a part of sadhana. If we want to eliminate the enemies that lurk at the innermost depths of your heart, we have to perform service to the world. Only then we can tell how effective our meditation has been. Only when some one gets angry at us, we will know whether there is anger in us still. The jackal thinks, as he sits alone in the forest, 'Now I am strong; I will not howl when I see a dog next time.' But as soon as he sees a dog, he forgets everything and starts howling loudly. When we mingle with people, we have to stay above anger in circumstances where they get angry. Only then, we can understand the extent of our growth.

"You might rank high in the school exams, but that may not get you a job. To qualify for the job, you have to secure a high rank in the test taken by thousands people applying for it. You have to get a good rank in that test. Only then you will qualify for the job. Similarly, after your meditations take you to some level, you should work for society. Only when you have the strength to withstand the ridicule and abuse heaped on you, Amma will say that you have become complete.

"Even an inexperienced driver may be able to drive a car through an empty meadow. The true test of someone's driving skill is his ability to drive safely through crowded streets. Likewise, you cannot call someone courageous just because he sits in solitude and does spiritual practices. The truly courageous person is one who can go forward without faltering the least in the midst of adversity as he engages in a variety of tasks. He is the true sage and no circumstance destroys the poise of his mind.

"Thus, service should be seen as sadhana. It should be done as an offering to God. Then if someone opposes us, we might feel a little hostility, but we can get rid of it through contemplation. 'Who was the object of my hostility? Didn't I get angry at him because I took myself to be the body? What have I learnt from the scriptures? Which world am I traveling to? How could I feel ill will towards him even after declaring that I am not the body or mind, but the soul! Who in him was the object of my anger?' We should do this type of self-examination repeatedly. Eventually, we will stop feeling anger towards anyone. We will feel remorse and it will lead us on the right path."

Br: "If we don't say a word in response when others show their hostility, aren't we giving them the opportunity to err and to use foul language? Is it right on such occasions to stay quiet, imagining we are the atman? Won't they take our patience only as a weakness?"

Non-duality in daily life

Mother: "We should see everything as Brahman; but we should use our discrimination also to act properly in each circumstance. As we stand on the road side, a dog comes running our way, followed by a crowd shouting, 'Here comes a mad dog!' The rabid dog has no discrimination. It will bite us if we remain in its way. We should move aside. Perhaps we should even carry a stick. Mother won't advice that we should close our eyes to this threat. But we shouldn't beat the dog unnecessarily. It doesn't know right or wrong. We should deny it a chance to bite us by getting out of its way. We should see the dog and the people who warned us all as Brahman. In stead of that, if we ignore the warning to get out of the way and stay in front of the dog thinking it is Brahman, we will surely get bitten. There is no point in feeling sorry later.

"We should use our discrimination in every circumstance, children! A spiritual seeker should never be a weak person. Take a little boy, our Sivan (Amma's nephew), for instance. He makes many mistakes and we may spank him a lot. But we have no animosity towards him; we are not spanking him out of revenge. He is a small boy. We know that he is making mistakes out of ignorance. But only if we wield the stick today, he will be careful tomorrow. So we put on a show of anger. That is the attitude we should have. We should, of course, rein in those who act without discrimination. But we shouldn't lose our own equanimity while doing so. Even as we show our displeasure outwardly, we should love them inside. We should wish that they become good. Only then we can make progress.

"Like a lion outside, but like a flower inside - that is how a sadhak should be. His heart should be like a full blossom; it should never wither. But outside, he should be brave and strong as a lion. Only then he will be able to guide the world. But while doing sadhana, he should be like the lowliest of servants. Take a beggar who begs for food, but walks away without getting angry even if he is given nothing but abuse. A seeker should assume the attitude of such a beggar. Only then he will be able to grow. Children, only a brave person can be patient. The beggar-like attitude during sadhana will actually strengthen his courage. The seed of courage will sprout only in the soil of patience".

The aged 'Unnikkannan' ('baby Krishna', as Amma called Ottoor) sat on his bed, leaning forward, his face beaming with joy as he took in the sweet nectar of words flowing from Amma. When he saw Amma getting up to leave, he bowed to Her from where he sat and offered Her a packet containing sugar that had been offered to the Lord in the Guruvayur temple. (Ottoor was associated with the Guruvayur temple all his life. He always kept with him some of the prasad from there). Mother gave him the first chance to enjoy the prasad from the packet, placing a little of the sugar on his tongue that was blessed through years of chanting of the name of the Lord.

Tuesday, September 24, 1985

A cooking lesson

It was after five in the evening. A brahmacharini was cutting vegetables for dinner. In between she got up frequently to keep the cooking fire going. Mother saw this as She came in to the kitchen. "Daughter, you can go and take care of the fire. Amma will do this!," She said. She sent the brahmacharini to tend the fire and started to cut the vegetables. Seeing Amma engaged in this task, several others joined Her.

Mother: "Children, that daughter was struggling alone here. She had to cut the vegetables and keep the stoves going at the same time. None of you came to help! As soon as Amma came, all of you have come running to help. Children, sadhana does not mean sitting idly somewhere. You should feel compassion when you see others struggling. You should feel the urge to help. You do sadhana to acquire a mind filled with compassion. Once you have that, you have everything. When Amma is on the scene, everyone comes running! That is not true devotion towards Her. One who is able to love everyone equally is the one who truly loves Amma."

A brahmachari: "Mother, the other day I came to the kitchen to help. But I ended up being scolded."

Mother: "You must have done some mischief."

Br: "It seems that I had cut the vegetables into pieces that were too large."

Mother and the others laugh. Mother called the brahmacharini.

Mother (still laughing): "Did you scold this son the other day, even though he was here to help?"

Bri: "It is true that he came to help. But in the end, my work only doubled! I told him to chop the vegetables into small pieces. He made very large pieces and I had to cut each piece again. It took twice as long! I did tell him then that he need not come to help again, if this was what he would do."

Mother: "But he is not used to this; isn't it why he did that? Shouldn't you show him how you wanted it done? He is not used to cutting vegetables. He hasn't done any work at home."

Mother explained to everyone how to cut vegetables properly and what one needs to pay attention to. By the time the cooking lesson was over, the vegetables had all been chopped. A brahmacharini brought some water. Mother washed Her hands and left the kitchen.

Mother blesses a cow

Mother walked to the cowshed. Those who followed Her saw an astonishing sight.

Mother was kneeling near a cow and drinking milk directly from her udders! The cow let the milk flow generously. When Amma left one nipple and started to suck another one, milk was dripping onto Her face. The eyes of the mother cow, who had the great good fortune to suckle the Mother of the World, seemed to say, 'All my tapas was for this one moment! Now my birth has been fulfilled!'

Mother came out, wiping Her face with the end of her sari. Seeing all Her children gathered there, She said, 'That cow has been wishing to give milk to Amma for a long time!'

The Mother who fulfills the silent wishes of even the cows! Those cows were indeed blessed souls who had accrued much merit. How else would they come to have such a wish?

Mother continued: "Long ago, when Amma's family and the neighbors were against Her, the animals and birds came to Her help. It is out of Her own experience that Amma says that if you surrender totally to God, He will make sure that you don't lack anything. When there was no one to feed Her, the dog would bring a packet of rice from somewhere, holding the packet between its teeth. Sometimes She wouldn't have eaten for days. After meditation, She would lie unconscious in the sand somewhere. When She opened Her eyes, She would see one of the cows standing next to Her, with her udders full of milk ready for Her to drink. Amma would drink as much as She wanted. That cow would come and offer milk whenever Amma felt tired."

The devotees, who always regretted that they were not around to witness those *leelas*, at least had the good fortune to witness this scene today.

Worshipping the deities and the Guru

As Amma was walking to the ashram, a brahmachari asked: "Amma, do deities really exist?"

Mother: "They exist in the subtle plane, son. Each deity represents a characteristic that is latent in us. But you should view your chosen deity as indistinct from the Supreme Self.

God can assume any form He chooses. Doesn't the ocean rise up in response to the attraction exerted by the moon? The Lord will assume many forms depending on the desire of the devotee."

Br: "Amma, rather than worships the deities whom we have never seen, isn't it best to take refuge in the mahatmas who are alive amongst us?"

Mother: "Yes. A real *tapasvi* has the power to assume the burden of our prarabdha. If we take refuge in a mahatma with devotion our prarabdhas will end soon. We need to put in more effort to benefit from worship of deities or from temple worship."

Amma continued after pausing for a moment: "If we worship our chosen deity with the attitude that he is the Supreme Self, we can indeed attain self-realization. A form is like a ladder. All forms will merge in the formless eventually, just as all shadows disappear at high noon. But if we take refuge in a satguru, the path will be easier. A guru's help is necessary to remove the obstacles in sadhana and to show us the way. Gurus can help us by clearing our doubts in all crises. Then the journey will be easier. A child can do whatever he wants if the mother is holding his hand. He won't fall even if he takes both feet off the ground. But the child shouldn't try to free himself from the grasp of the mother. He should let his mother guide him. Or else he will fall down. Likewise, a guru will always come to the aid of the disciple."

A devotee: "Is meditating on a mahatma equal to meditating on the Self?"

Mother: "If we view a mahatma in the proper light, we can reach Brahman. In reality, mahatmas don't have a form. If we make a bitter melon out of chocolate, it will still be sweet. Mahatmas who have attained full knowledge of the Self are the same as Brahman who has assumed a form. All their forms and moods are sweet."

Br: "Some people meditate on Amma, others on Kali. Is their any real difference between these two?"

Mother: "If you look at the real essence, what is the difference? Whatever form you meditate on, the important thing is your *sankalpa*, what you attribute to the form. You will get the result appropriate to that. Some people meditate on certain deities and obtain siddhis; they do this for achieving certain results. Their concept of the deitiy's form is a very limited one. We should see the deity in *tattva* (the principle behind the deity). Only then we can go beyond the form, beyond the limits. We have to appreciate that everything is the all-pervading Self. We have to see the deity of our worship as the undivided Self. It is only a difference in sankalpa. People sometimes worship a deity in the course of certain observances or rituals. That involves only the concept of a deity, not of God.

"All forms have limits. No tree touches the heavens. No root reaches the netherworld. We are trying to reach the Supreme Self. When we get on the bus we are not planning to live in it, do we? Our aim is to reach home. The bus will take us to our gate. It is our job to walk from the gate to the house. Deities will bring us to the doorway to the Supreme *Sat-chit-ananda*. From there, it is not far to Self-realization.

"Even those who have transcended all limitations do not forsake their hold on a form. It is said that even jivanmuktas - those who have attained liberation in this life - crave to hear the name of the Lord."

Amma's memorable words imparting the subtle aspects of sadhana shed new light in the minds of the listeners. Everyone bowed to Her with a sense of fulfillment and returned to their normal duties.

Sunday, October 13, 1985

> *One who sees every being in himself and sees himself in everything else does not shrink with aversion from anything thereafter - Isavasya Upanishad.*

Mother is getting ready to empty and clean the septic tank attached to the guest house toilet. The tank is full. She has just returned from a day-long journey and bhajan and darshan. The moment She is back, She wants to take up the scavenger's job. Not that Her children were unwilling to do this job. In fact, they had requested Amma to stand aside. But She insists on setting an example and does not normally ask someone else to do a job.

Mother: "A mother does not mind cleaning up the excreta of her baby - because she has the sense of 'mineness' towards the baby. But we should have that same *prema* towards every one. Then we wouldn't feel any aversion or disgust."

The excitement of working with Mother is something special. It is an intoxication. Everyone is yearning to work alongside Her even if it is hard toil. They don't ask whether they are dealing with sand or cement or feces!

"In the old days, there were no lavatory facilities for those who came for darshan. That meant that the first job of Amma's oldest children in the morning was to cleanup the ashram surroundings!" Mother recalled the early days: "There were no fences separating the adjacent properties. So, most of the time we ended up cleaning the neighbors' property also!"

A brahmachari was handling the buckets filled with contents of the septic tank, taking care not to slosh or spill anything. As buckets began to be passed rapidly, his attention wavered and one bucket fell to the ground. The excreta splashed all over his body.

Mother: "Don't worry, son! We carry all this inside us, after all! It will wash off. The real dirt is the attitude that 'I am the doer' while doing anything - whether it is puja or cleaning the gutter. That is hard to wash away. You should learn to consider any work you do as an offering to God, my children! Only then the inside will be clean. That is why Amma is making you do all this. Amma doesn't want Her darling children to be ones who stand apart and order others to do such work. A brahmachari should be fit to do any work."

Not only the brahmacharis, but some of the devotees also were taking part in the work. One devotee who was awakened by all the noise and light came out to find out what was going on. When he saw what Mother was doing, he could not stand apart. He took off his shirt, tucked up his dhoti and got ready to get into the septic tank.

Mother: "No, son. The work is almost done. There is no need for you too to have to take a bath at night."

But who is listening to Her? The devotee said, his lips quivering with emotion: "Will you give that bucket to me and move out of the way, Amma?"

Amma smiled, hearing in his voice the sense of authority arising out of love.

"*Mone*, Amma doesn't feel any aversion in cleaning up the excreta of Her devotees. It is a pleasure," She said.

"Don't go after that pleasure now. Will you give this to me?" He said in a choking voice, trying to grab the bucket from Amma's hands.

Often, we see the devotees taking a level liberty with Mother that the inmates of the ashram would hesitate to take. Amma will yield only to pure, unblemished devotion.

It was the auspicious hour before dawn when the work was finished. To those who observed the life in this ashram it seemed as if one had to amend the statement in the Gita, 'That which is night for all beings, in that the yogin keeps awake'. Here night was day even for those who chose to be with the yogin.

Saturday, October 19, 1985

Follow the principle behind rituals

Mother came down to the kalari a while ago. The brahmacharis and some householder devotees were there with Her. It was not yet time for the bhajan.

The relative who stayed at the ashram to take care of Ottoor was ill. Some of the brahmacharis were taking care of Ottoor. In the matter of rituals, Ottoor was usually very particular. It was difficult to please him. When the conversation turned to that subject, Amma said:

"Mother doesn't know about *acharas*[13]. She didn't grow up

---

[13] Customary observances, rituals.

observing them. But Damayanti Amma was very strict. She didn't allow friendship with anybody. There was one benefit from that. When you are alone, you can sing hymns in praise of God. You can talk to Him. You waste time in idle talk only if you have some one else with you. A speck of dust in one of the washed utensils was enough to make Damayanti Amma spank Her. There shouldn't be even a tiny shred of anything left in the yard after it was swept. If there was, Damayanti Amma would beat Her with the broom until the broom itself was broken. (Laughing) May be it is this upbringing that has made Amma so strict with Her children now. She is a terror now, isn't She?

"In those days, after She swept the front yard, She would stand in one corner, imagining that the Lord was walking in front of Her. She would imagine seeing each one of his footsteps in the sand as He walked. Whatever She did, there was only the thought of God.

"Whatever you are engaged in, there should be only thoughts about of God, children. That is the purpose of rituals. Rituals would help foster good habits. There will be order in life. But one should go beyond rituals. One should not be bound to them till death!"

A brahmachari: " Isn't it true that rituals cause the mind to flow only outward, but not towards God?"

Mother: "Every ritual started as an aid to maintain an unbroken remembrance of God. But it turned into a mere routine gradually.

"Haven't you heard this story? There was a priest. His cat used to bother him while he did his puja. Because of this annoyance, one day he put the cat under a basket before the puja started, and freed him afterwards. Soon, this became a habit. He would put the cat under a basket before starting the puja. His son used to help him do this. In due course, the old priest died and the son took over the responsibility for the puja. He didn't forget to put the cat under a basket before starting the worship. After some time, the cat also died. The next day when the time for puja came, the son was very worried. How could he start the puja without putting the cat under the basket? He ran out and got the neighbor's cat, put him under a basket and proceeded. Soon, he got a new cat, just for the puja, as it was hard to get the neighbor's cat, on time, every day. He did not know why his father put the cat under a basket, and he had never asked. He just copied everything his father had done. It shouldn't be like that. We should perform *acharas* only after grasping the principle behind them. Only then, we will benefit from them. Otherwise they will deteriorate into mere routines.

"We should be able to maintain the thought of God in all our actions. For example, before we sit down somewhere, we should touch our seat and bow to it, imagining our chosen deity in front. We should do the same thing as we get up. Whenever we pick up anything, we should show reverence this way, picturing the deity in it. Only if we maintain this alertness always, our minds will stay with God, without straying into worldly matters.

"Have you watched the mothers who work at the neighbor's house, leaving the babies at home? Whatever they are doing, their thoughts will be about the baby. Would he go near the well, would the other children hurt him in some way, would he go into the cowshed and go under the cows, or would he go near the kitchen fire? They will always be thinking like this. A sadhak should be the same way. He should be constantly thinking of God.

"The brahmacharis here haven't learnt any of the rituals. Serving people like him (meaning Ottoor), they will learn something. (Turning to the brahmachari) Son, even if he scolds you, you shouldn't be angry inside. If you feel anger, everything you did becomes a waste. You should consider any opportunity to serve a sadhu as a great blessing."

How to face blame and praise

A brahmachari complained to Amma about the character of one of the householder devotees. He sees the tiniest mistakes of the brahmacharis as very big and voices strong criticism, but doesn't see their good sides at all.

Mother: "Son, it is easy to like those who praise us. But we should really like even more those who point out our faults and shortcomings. They are the ones who really love us. When we see our mistakes, we can correct them and move ahead. We should see those who praise us as our enemies and those who deride us as our friends. We should keep this to ourselves; we need not show this to anyone. It is true that this is a very difficult attitude to cultivate. But we have set out to realize the Self, not to realize the body. Don't forget that!

"Praise and blame are all on the plane of the body, not on the plane of the Self. We should be able to see praise and blame as equal. We should learn not to lose our mental poise whether we get love or anger, praise or blame from others. That is real sadhana. We can progress upward only if we succeed in this."

Br: "Amma, why did you say that we should see as enemies those who praise us?"

Mother: "It means that they take us away from our goal. We should understand this and proceed with discrimination. It doesn't mean that we have to dislike anybody.

"All living beings look for the world of love. As long as we search for love outside, we fall into sorrow, just as fireflies perish in fire. All journeys that search for worldly love end in tears. That is the story of our lives now. Real love is not seen anywhere. There is only artificial love. It is like the light used by the fisherman. He spreads the net, turns on bright lights and waits. The fish come, attracted by the lights and soon the net is full. The fisherman fills his basket. Everyone loves from a selfish point of view.

"When others love us, we get close to them thinking that they will give us peace. But we don't see that the honey they offer us is a drop at the tip of a needle. If we try to enjoy that honey, the needle will pierce our tongues. Therefore, know the truth and go forward. Know that we have no friend but God. Then we won't have to be sorry."

The earth and sky bathed in the golden radiance of the evening sun. Soon the western sky turned deep red.

"The fishermen who go to sea would be very happy tonight," Mother said pointing to the glorious red color, "They say that means a big catch!"

The harmonium started playing. Amma took Her seat inside the kalari. Soon, She was withdrawn completely from the external world. She assumed the mood of the unalloyed devotion of a seeker in solitude. The bhajan started with *Kumbhodara varada...*

> *O Thou with a big belly,*
> *And the face of an elephant,*
> *Giver of boons, Son of Shiva,*
> *Lord of the Ganas...*
>
> *O Thou with five hands bestowing boons,*
> *Destroyer of sorrows,*
> *Son of Shiva, Bless us with Salvation.*
> *Let your benevolent glance fall on me!*
>
> *O Primal Lord, who takes us across*
> *The River of Samsara,*
> *Abode of mercy, Giver of Auspiciousness,*
> *O Hari, Nectar of Bliss, remover of obstacles,*
> *Show Thy compassion.*

The ashram and surroundings filled with the strains of the sweet devotional music. Everyone was immersed in the ecstasy of bhakti.

Sunday, October 20 1985

A mishap caused by a dog

"Children, We should love all living things, but that love should not cause harm to people. We are supposed to get out into the world and serve people. The compassion we show to one living being should not end up hurting another. If we are living in an isolated place, we can have dogs or cats or anything else. This is a place where a lot of people come and stay.

Children will try to play with the dog. It may bite them. It is better not to keep a dog in the ashram setting." A lot of people gathered around hearing Amma talking loudly.

Amma came down from Her room this morning hearing loud noises below. Amma's grandmother (whom She called Achamma, meaning father's mother) had gone behind the hut to get a long pole for picking flowers. Someone's dog had a litter of puppies recently and was nursing them behind the hut. The poor woman didn't know that. The dog in her agitation bit Achamma, who began to cry loudly. Brahmacharis and devotees had gathered around her by the time Mother came down.

Mother: "Poor thing, how would she go pick to flowers now. The dog has bitten deep."

Achamma was the one who gathered flowers daily from the neighborhood for the puja in the *kalari*. She would never break this routine however weak she felt. In the summer, she would often see in her dreams where she could find flowers. And her dream scenes were never wrong. She would get plenty of flowers in those places. And the neighbors usually did not object to her picking flowers there either.

The ashram residents began discussing the incident.

Br: Rao: "It is Unni who started keeping the dog here. He feeds it rice daily. So why would it leave the ashram?"

Mother: "Where is Unni? Call him."

Then She saw Unni standing behind Her.

Mother: "Is this your dog, son? Did you come here to rear dogs?"

Unni: "Amma, on a couple of days, as I was washing my hands after eating, I saw the dog waiting there. I felt sorry for it from the way it stood there."

Mother: "How many days have you fed it?"

Unni: "I have fed it occasionally. I didn't think it was going to deliver its puppies here."

Mother: "Does the dog need your permission to deliver?"

The brahmachari said, trying to suppress his laughter: "Amma, I felt sorry seeing its hungry look!"

Mother: "If you insisted on feeding it, take it far away somewhere and feed it. If you had done that, we wouldn't have this problem now."

She continued in a serious tone. "You felt sorry for the hungry dog. Don't you feel sorry now for this old grandmother who is standing here, bleeding from the dog's bite?

"We should see God in everything and offer our service, it is true. That is sadhana. We should show compassion for every living being. But there is a proper atmosphere for everything. This is not the place to keep cats and dogs. Does the poor animal know that this is an ashram or that Achamma is only trying to get the pole? You should get a spanking for keeping the dog here and feeding it!"

Amma took Unni's hands and held them together.

Unni: "Amma, I didn't feed it daily or anything. Just once in a while."

Mother: "No, don't say anything. I am going to tie you up today!"

She walked to the dining room without releasing him. Standing next to a pillar there, she asked a devotee to bring a rope. Knowing that all this was Her leela, the devotee brought a small piece of rope. When She saw the rope, Amma's mood changed. She said: "Well, not this one. This will hurt him if

Amma uses it. May be this time we will let him go!" She freed the brahmachari.

Dr. Leela[14] brought Achamma near Mother and said, "Amma, we don't know whether the dog is rabid or not. Shouldn't we give Achamma an injection?"

Mother: "The dog is not rabid or anything. You just apply some medicine to Achamma's wound, that is all."

Lot of devotees had arrived as it was a Sunday. When Amma reached the darshan hut, they crowded around Her. A female devotee whispered in Mother's ear: "I was scared by Amma's mood this morning!"

Amma laughed aloud and planted an affectionate kiss on her cheek. Those who are unfamiliar are bound to feel confused or awed when they see Mother chastising the brahmacharis. There will be such a seriousness on Her face on those occasions. But they will be surprised to see the nectar of love and affection flowing from Her the very next moment.

Amma is love itself. She does not know how to be angry. She knows only how to love.

The Mother who bestows unseen blessings

Mother asked a female devotee: "Daughter, Amma looked for you the other day. Why did you leave early?"

The other day as Amma came out of Her room, there was a packet containing some boiled *kachil* and seasoning just outside the door. Amma tasted a piece and asked a brahmacharini to go and get the woman who had brought the packet. The

---

[14] Now Swamini Atma Prana.

woman had apparently left and couldn't be found. No one knew who had left the packet at Amma's door.

Devotee: "I was very worried that day, Amma. The deal on a piece of property we were buying was to be closed on that day. I had promised to be at the court at eleven with the money. But, even after pawning my bangles and chain, we could not raise enough cash. We asked several people but no one helped. If the deed wasn't registered by eleven, we were going to lose the advance deposit we had made. I was very worried. Anyway, I thought I would come and see Ammachi in the morning. I brought some boiled kachil with me. It was nine-thirty when I got here. Someone told me that Amma will come out only later. If I got to the court before noon, I could ask for a refund of at least half of the deposit, even if the deal didn't go through. They might give it. So I left the packet at the door here and left. I cried a lot. I had hoped that with Amma's blessing, I will get at least half of the deposit back.

"When I got to Ochira, I saw an old friend of mine, waiting for the bus there. Her husband works in Saudi Arabia. Since I happened to meet her there, I thought I might as well ask her for help. I explained the situation. 'If I don't have ten thousand rupees before noon, the deal will collapse,' I told her. By Amma's grace, she had exactly that much money with her! She had just been paid back a loan she had made to someone, and she was on her back after collecting the money. She gave the money without a word. I just broke into tears! And the deal went through, just by Ammachi's grace!"

The woman's eyes were full. Amma embraced her tightly and wiped her tears with Her sari.

The treasure inside

There was going to be a puja in a devotee's house. The brahmachari who was to do it came to get Mother's blessing before going there.

Mother blessed him and said: "Son, there is an anthill in their place. They are guarding it, following someone's advice that it should not be destroyed. Amma doesn't think it is very important. Even if we do all the right things, if the devotees don't have proper faith and a sense of surrender, they will not get the benefit. Some people may blindly believe in some thing. They won't budge from it, however much we explain things to them. Then, we have to get down to their level and do what is needed. Whatever gives them peace is what is appropriate now. That does not mean that we leave them to their blind beliefs. Therefore you should tell them, 'This anthill will not bring you any harm. But there is no need to leave it like this. Keep just a small piece of it in your puja room. You can destroy the rest. If it keeps growing here, you will just waste that much space.' At the end of the puja, you take a little of the sand from the anthill and give it to them to keep in the puja room."

Mother told the devotees around her: "Once somebody came here with a similar story. There was an anthill near his house. An astrologer convinced him that there was a treasure under it and that he could recover it if he did some pujas. He sought the help of countless astrologers and others to extract the treasure. Many of them promised to help him and took a lot of his money, but he didn't get any treasure. Finally he came here. His only question was when he will get the treasure, not whether there was a treasure at all. What could Amma say?

He was angry at Her for telling him that there was no treasure. 'All the astrologers I saw said there was a treasure. If you can't see even that, why should I come here'. He said this and left. His mind was full of the dream of treasure. What could we do? Amma told him that there was no treasure, but he couldn't accept that.

"But soon he came back. He had an experience that brought him back. (She laughs) Now he is interested in the treasure within, not in the treasure outside. If we had rejected him completely in the beginning, his future would have been dark. Therefore, when such people come, we should find out the level of their understanding, and go to that level first. And gradually we should bring spiritual ideas and viewpoints to them.

"Everyone wants the treasure outside. They are willing to go to any amount of trouble for that. Nobody wants the treasure within. We have a treasure within us which we will never lose, which no one can steal. But we will not get it by searching outside. We have to look inside. We have to offer the flower of our heart to the Lord."

The devotees watched as Mother gave a them a sweet smile to keep in their hearts and climbed the steps to Her room. Some of them may have wondered what the flower of the heart fit to offer Her would be like.

> *The flower that is not caressed by the rays of the sun,*
> *The flower that is not stolen by the wind in stealth*
> *The mind is that flower – it is a full blossom.*

The mind not stained at all by desire,
The mind that doesn't throw flames of anger,
The flower that is not offered in love to a maiden,
That is the mind the Divine Empress dwells in.

The mind that gives your life its full of meaning,
The mind that yearns for the welfare of others,
The mind that is filled with love unblemished,
That mind is worn as a garland by Mother!

The strength you seek is right within you,
Give up this tottering search, O my mind!
Go forward boldly to the goal of your life,
As selfishness fades, there Mother will shine.

When all is surrendered, there is a soul,
Free of false pride, filled with peace.
That is a light that can't be captured in words,
There Mother Divine will dance forever!

As they stood there cherishing Amma's sweet smile, they recalled this song that She often sang about the flower to be offered to the Divine Mother.

Wednesday, October 23, 1985

Initiation from the Goddess of learning

It was Vijaya Dashami day. Devotees started arriving early in the morning, with little children who were to receive their first lessons from the Goddess of Learning Herself. Most of them were mothers from the nearby coastal areas. People from far away had arrived two days earlier and were staying at the ashram. Mother came to the meditation room with some of the children who had already placed their books in the pile at the spot where the puja to Sarasvati, the Goddess of Learning was performed. Many devotees had already taken their seats in the room. There was a festive atmosphere at the ashram.

There was not enough space in the meditation room for everybody at the same time. "Little children come first!" Amma called.

Children gathered around the pile of books, holding tulsi leaves in their hands.

"Om mushika vahana modaka hasta..."
"Om Sarasvati namasthubhyam..."

Many tender voices echoed the mantras praising Lord Ganesha and Devi Sarasvati that Amma recited line by line.

Mother: "Now all of you children, imagine that you see your favorite deity in front of you. Kiss those divine feet and prostrate!"

Mother prostrated first. The children did the same thing. Many more children were waiting outside.

The brahmacharis sat down on the south side of the room to start the bhajan. Amma took Her seat on the north side with a plate full of rice in which the letters of the alphabet were about to blossom from the finger tips of the waiting children. The parents took their turn and brought their children to Her so that she could guide their first steps into the world of knowledge. She put the children on Her lap, one by one, and calmed them with a piece of candy. Every one in the room watched with fascination as Mother guided the tender fingers of the children and made them write a few letters in the rice.

"Hari!," Amma says. The little child sitting in Her lap, decked in his new gilded *mundu* and wearing sandal paste on his forehead, looks up at Her face, wondering what is going on!

Mother prods him: " 'Hari!', say it, 'Ha ri!'"

The child faithfully repeats, "Hari, say it, Hari!" Everyone including Mother bursts into laughter.

Many of the children start to cry as they come to Her. But She wouldn't let any of them go without making them write in the rice. Meanwhile, the bhajan in praise of the Goddess of Learning echoes the sentiment in the hearts of the parents:

> *'O Sarasvati, Goddess of all learning,*
> *Give us your blessings!*
> *Scholars we are not,*
> *Dull-witted we are,*
> *Just puppets in your hands!'*

Mother does not like Her children giving Her a *dakshina* (a traditional offering made to some one conducting a worship or ceremony). But the parents wanted their children to give Her something on this occasion. Many poor parents from the coastal area had brought their children. They were unable to offer anything comparable to what many others could. To make sure that they didn't feel hurt, Amma decided that it was enough if every one offered just one rupee to honor the custom, and that was to be placed in front of the picture of Sarasvati. She did not want any of the mothers to feel sorry that their children could not offer a dakshina equal to others.

It was eleven by the time all the little children were initiated into the alphabet. Mother came out into the yard. The householders and brahmacharis were sitting there in lines. Mother also sat down with them. Amma called out, "Om." Every one repeated the primordial syllable and wrote it in the sand,

"Om."

"*Hari Shri Ganapataye Namah*!", the lesson continued... Finally, to enhance the sweetness of the lesson in words, all the devotees also received prasad from Amma's hands.

By noon, a good number of the visitors went home happily. After receiving instruction from the Mother of all learning, the brahmacharis sat here and there, repeating their lessons or reciting Vedic mantras. Unable so far to unload their burden of sorrows in Mother's lap, many devotees waited with anxious eyes. The tireless Amma gathered them all and went to the darshan hut.

Give to those who are in need

Janakiyamma, from the town of Pandalam, was talking to Mother. She was a retired teacher, who came frequently to see Mother. She was worried about the ways of her oldest son.

Mother: "How is your son now?"

Janaki: "You should straighten him out, Amma! I can't. What can I do if someone his age cannot look after his own life?"

Mother: "That is what happens when you show too much affection towards children."

Janaki: "He has plenty of time for his friends and

neighbors. If anyone talks to him about their money problems, he is ready to help, even if that means robbing our house. I am retired now. It is sad if he does not look after himself at least from now on. What does he get for giving away like this? Tomorrow none of these people will even recognize us if we go to them for help."

Mother: "When we give, we should know to whom we are giving. We should give where there is need. And, we should give without wishing for anything in return. If we give to get something in return, wouldn't that be just a sale, daughter?

"We should recognize the needy and help them. We should give to those who have lost their health and can't work any more, those who are handicapped, little children who have been abandoned by their parents, those who are sick, but don't have the resources for treatment, those who are old and have no family to help them. That is our *dharma* and we should not expect anything in return for our help. But we should think twice before giving to those who are healthy and are able to work. If we give money to them, they become lazier. And when many people give, won't they have a lot of money? They will waste it on alcohol and drugs. If that happens, we are the ones who accrue the sin from their actions. If we didn't give them money, they wouldn't have committed any of those mistakes.

"We can give a share of our food to those who are hungry. We can give medicines to the sick. We can give clothes to those who need protection from the cold. If someone can't find a regular job, we can make them do some work and then give some financial help. If we become poor by giving away money to others thoughtlessly, we can't blame God for that.

"It is all right to give money to ashrams and other

institutions which serve the world. They will not waste that money. Institutions like ashrams spend money on morally sound projects. But even in this case, we should not give just to get name and fame. We should see it as an opportunity to serve God. The merit from giving a gift will come to us, in any event. When we make a gift, only we should know about it. Isn't there a saying that the left hand shouldn't know what the right hand gives?"

Mother wiped the woman's tears and hugged her, and consoled her saying: "Stop worrying, daughter! Amma is here for you!"

Janaki: "Amma, let him give everything away to whomever he wants. I have no complaints. But I don't have the strength to see him beg for small change some day. You should take me away before then, Amma!"

Mother: "Don't cry daughter! You will never have to see that. You will never lack anything. Isn't Amma with you always?" Amma hugged her again, and gave her a kiss.

No poverty for the true devotee

As soon as the woman withdrew from Amma with a peaceful smile brought on by Her kiss, the next devotee, a man named Divakaran, was in Her lap.

Mother: "When did you come, son? Amma didn't see you while giving prasadam to everyone."

Divakaran: "I wanted to come in the morning, Amma! But the bus was late and I got here only now."

Mother: "There was another *mon* with you last time."

Divakaran: "Yes, that was Bhaskaran. He is always in

difficulty, Amma. He has been going to the temple at Sabarimala regularly for the last seventeen years. There are very few temples that he doesn't visit. His poverty and other problems still haunt him, as much as ever. When I see his case, I even wonder why we should think of God!"

Mother: "Son, if we take refuge in God fully, only good things will happen to us, materially and spiritually. There is no record of a mahatma starving to death. The whole world has come down to its knees in front of them. Someone who takes ultimate refuge in God will not have to suffer from poverty. The main reason for our present sorrows is that we don't surrender fully to God. Our devotion is not for its own sake; it is for fulfilling our desires. The desires lead to sorrow."

Another devotee: "Didn't Kuchela[15] have firm devotion for the Lord? Still he had to suffer poverty."

Mother: "It is not right to say that Kuchela suffered because of his poverty. How could he find time to experience any sorrow, immersed as he was constantly in thoughts about God? His unalloyed devotion gave him the ability to remain blissful even in the midst of poverty. Because of his surrender to God, even the poverty, which was a part of his prarabdha, disappeared. Kuchela did not collapse under the weight of poverty, nor did he forget God in an excess of joy, when all the riches came to him.

"If we take refuge in God, without any desires, He will give us everything we need, as we need it. And when we surrender to Him with the attitude that He will take care of everything, then we don't need to fear anything. There will be prosperity

---

[15] A great devotee of Lord Krishna whose story appears in the Shrimad Bhagavatam.

and happiness everywhere. The Goddess of Prosperity will be the servant of one who has pure devotion. But what kind of devotion do we have now? We say we go to the temple; but no one goes there just to see the Lord. Even in his sacred presence, we talk only of worldly affairs. What is the need of going to the temple if all we do is talk about our family and neighbors? At least when we are in the temple, we should meditate solely on the Lord, surrendering all our burdens to Him, realizing that He is aware of all our problems without being told. We should not go to the temple just to voice our complaints. We should go to worship and strengthen the remembrance of God in us."

At this stage of the conversation, some of the other devotees, who were silent till then, started asking questions.

Put your faith into action

A devotee: "But, Amma, you yourself have said that we should open our hearts and tell everything to God."

Mother: "Don't we get some relief when we confide our problems to those who are dear to us? We should feel that same love and nearness to God. We have to feel that He is our own. We need not hide anything from Him. It is in that sense that Amma says we should tell Him everything. It is good to lighten the burden in our hearts by telling God about all our sorrows. We should depend only on Him in all our difficulties. The true devotee cannot tell anyone else about his troubles; God is his only real relative. But there is no use going to God with our hearts filled only with desires and family problems.

"We have to explain the background of the case to the lawyer; only then he can argue for us. Similarly, we have to describe our disease to the doctor; only then he can treat us. But we don't have to go into the details to let God know about our problems. He knows about everything. He dwells within us, watching every movement of ours. Only His power enables us to see and hear and act. Only through His power we can know Him. We can see the sun only because of his light. What we have to do therefore, is to surrender everything to the Lord, and to remember Him constantly.

"Our strongest relation should be with Him. If we decide to tell Him about our sorrows, it should only be for getting closer to Him. It is our faith and surrender to God or Guru that removes our sorrows. Just describing our difficulties will not be of any use."

The brahmachari sitting nearby raised a doubt: "Amma, is it possible to attain self-realization just by faith in God?"

Mother: "If you have total faith, that itself is realization. But we don't have that. Therefore, we certainly have to strive for it and do sadhana. It is not enough to have faith in the doctor. We have to take the medicine to get cured. Likewise, both faith and effort are needed. If you plant a seed, it will sprout. But, for it to grow well, it needs water and fertilizer. Faith will make us aware of our true nature; but, to experience it directly, we need to put out the effort.

"There is a story about a father and his son. The son had a disease and the doctor prescribed the extract from a certain plant as the cure. They searched for the plant everywhere, but couldn't find it. They walked around for a long time and became very tired and thirsty. They saw a well and approached it. They found a rope and a bucket near the well. Many wild plants grew nearby. As he put the bucket in the well to draw water, the father noticed, at the bottom of the well, the medicinal plant they were searching for everywhere. He tried to get down into the well, but couldn't. There were no steps, and the well was very deep. The father didn't hesitate any longer. He tied the rope to his son's waist and lowered him carefully into the well. 'Pull up the plants carefully when you get down there', he told the boy. Some travelers happened to come that way at that moment. They were amazed at the man's action. 'What kind of a man are you who puts this little boy into the well at the end of a rope?', they asked. The father kept silence. The boy reached the bottom of the well and pulled up the plants carefully. The father raised him slowly. When he got out of the well, the others asked, 'But how did you get the courage to go down into the well at the end of a rope?' The son answered without hesitation, 'It was *my father* who held the rope!'

"The son had deep faith in his father. But only when he put that into action, by going down into the well and getting the medicine, he got the benefit of his faith. Children, that is the form of faith we need in God. 'God is there to protect me. Then why should I grieve? I am not even worried about self realization!' We have to have such a sense of assurance. The devotion of one who is plagued by doubts at every moment is not devotion; his faith is not true faith."

Faith in God and faith in oneself

A young man: "Mother, what is the need to depend on God? Isn't it enough to rely on self effort? After all, we have all the powers within us. Aren't all the gods created by man?"

Mother: "Son, now we live with the attitude of 'I' and

'mine'. As long as this attitude exists, we will not be able to find the power within us. When there is a curtain across the window, we cannot see the sky. Pull the curtain to a side, and the sky will be visible. Similarly, only if we remove the sense of 'I' from our minds, we can see the light within us. And that sense cannot be removed without humility and dedication.

"To build a canoe, the wood is heated in the fire, so that it can be bent into the right shape. We may say that this takes the wood to its true form. Similarly, our humility reveals our true form.

"If a thread is fat or out of shape, it will not pass through the eye of the needle. It has to shrink to a sleek form, before it can pass through. But that surrender on its part enables it sew countless pieces of cloth together. Similarly, surrender is the principle that brings the individual self (jivatman) to the Supreme Self (paramatman). All this is within us, but in order to bring it out we need to do put forth ceaseless effort. We may have a musical talent, but only if we practice regularly, we can sing in a way that gives pleasure to the listeners. What we have within us needs to be brought to the plane of experience. There is no use saying, 'Everything is in me.' We take pride in our status and position and our abilities, but we falter when adverse circumstances arise. We lose the faith in ourselves. Constant effort is needed to change this.

"We think that everything works because of our powers. But without the Lord's power, we are just inert bodies. We boast that we can burn the whole world down by pushing a button. But don't we need to move the finger to push that button? Where do we get the power to do that?

"There are road signs written with special luminous paint.

They glow when the light from approaching vehicles falls on them. This helps the drivers to get information about their route and road conditions. But imagine a road sign thinking, 'Those cars run because of my light. Can they find their way without me?' When we say 'my power' or 'my ability' it is similar to that. The sign glows only when the cars' light falls on it. In the same way, we are able to move and to act only because of the Almighty's grace and His power. He is the one who protects us always. If we surrender to Him, He will guide us always. If we have that faith, we will never falter."

It is noon. Mother has not eaten anything today. She is with Her children since very early in the morning. This is the story everyday. Many prostrations to this embodiment of selflessness, who sees the whole world as Her children and showers Her affection on all constantly!

CHAPTER FIVE

Friday, October 25, 1985

The Mother who showers Her blessings

Sethuraman and his family came forward and prostrated to Amma. Sethu works in Assam. After his college, he could not get a job for several years. It was when he was getting desperate that he came to see Mother for the first time. She gave him a mantra and asked him to chant it a hundred and eight times daily and do archana. He followed Mother's instructions to the letter. Three weeks later, his uncle who worked in Assam came home on vacation. He promised to arrange a job for his nephew. Sethu left for Assam soon afterwards and is now back home on vacation. His wife is also with him. She was a coworker whom he married with the concurrence of his family and with Amma's blessings. Amma Herself had conducted the naming ceremony for their first-born girl, Soumya. Amma welcomed Sethu's wife and baby into Her arms while Her face beamed with the happiness of a matriarch who welcomes her young daughter-in-law into the family. Sethu stood by, as tears of happiness welled up in his eyes.

Mother: "Aren't you staying till tomorrow, children?"

Sethu: "We were thinking of leaving right away after seeing you, Amma, but we have decided to stay here tonight."

Mother (to the brahmachari standing near Her): "Give your room to them, son!" She said to Sethu, "Amma will see you after the bhajan."

The brahmacharis had taken their seats already. The bhajan started soon.

Prapanchamengum...

O Illusory Appearance
That fills the whole Universe,
O Radiance, won't you
Dawn in my heart and stay there
Shedding Thy Light forever?

I will surfeit myself
Drinking Thy motherly Love,
Coming near Thee and
Sinking in Thy Divine effulgence
All my distress will flee!

How long have I wandered
Searching Thou, the Core
Of everything; O Mother,
Won't Thou come before me,
Grant me the bliss of the Self,
O won't Thou come?

The stars were shining brightly. Amma started digging under some *chembu* plants. There was no bulb to be found. She Herself had dug up everything on several occasions previously. The strains of the hymns from the kalari floated in the air. Amma had come out of the kalari and gone to the northern side of the ashram, at the end of a kirtan She was singing. This happened occasionally. If She got too absorbed in the singing and felt that She couldn't hold Herself down on this plane, She would try to bind Her mind in some work She has often said: "Amma can't sing even one line with total attention, children! She would lose Her grip! So, when She sings one line, She would try consciously to remember the next one. She wonders how Her children can sing bhajans without crying!"

After digging up a lot of roots, Mother had found a handful of edible bulbs. She washed them, put them in a pot with some water, made a fire and started cooking them. They were only half-cooked, when Amma put a hot piece in her mouth. She gave the rest to Her children and went to Her room.

Amma's prasad, in the form of half-cooked, unsalted, unseasoned pieces of *chembu*, which resembled little sparrow's eggs! As Her children walked to the kalari, holding the prasad in their hands, just in time for the arati at the end of the bhajan, what Amma had said on an earlier occasion blossomed in their minds like a flower of the night: "My children, do you know how much effort Amma has to make to stay here in your world?"

It was an hour after midnight. Mother came down from Her room. A brahmachari was doing japa in the kalari. Seeing Amma in front of him unexpectedly, he prostrated at Her feet. Mother asked him to call everybody. Everybody felt wide awake hearing that Amma was calling, and rushed to Her side, not knowing the reason. She asked them to bring something to sit on and started walking to the sea side.

Everyone now knew it was time for meditation. Mother

took the brahmacharis to the sea shore occasionally to meditate. There was no fixed time for this. It could be at any hour. Everyone sat around Amma on the beach. All quiet, except for the deep 'Om...' sound of the sea - and the incessant crashing of the waves on the shore. The lights on the fishing boats twinkled, far away in the sea. Amma chanted Om thrice. Every one echoed that. She said, "If anybody is sleepy, stand up and chant your mantra. If you are still sleepy, run along the beach for a little while and sit down again. This hour, when the whole Nature is very quiet, is the best time for meditation."

Two hours passed very quickly. At the end Mother chanted Om again which everyone repeated. Following Her instruction, they imagined their chosen deity in front and prostrated. Amma sang a hymn in praise of the Divine Mother.

Sri chakram ennoru...

The moonlight lit up the sea. The horizon was partly hidden by a thin curtain of mist. A few isolated stars shone above. Even the waves seemed to try to be quiet. The white-robed singers on the beach were like a flock of swans who had descended to rest for a while on the shores of time, at the twilight of some ancient epoch. Amma's form glowed in their minds like the white mountain reflected on the still waters of the Manasa Lake[16].

---

[16] Manasa Lake ('Lake of the Mind', believed to be created by the mind of Lord Brahma) is in the Kailasa Mountain in the Himalayas. It is said to be the birthplace of swans.

Tuesday, October 29, 1985

Mother drinks poisoned milk

Mother called all the brahmacharis to her room in the afternoon. She was sitting in the middle of the room. There were many packets in front of Her, containing a variety of sweets.

Mother: "Amma wanted to give you children these things for some time. She didn't get time to do it so far."

She gave each person some sweets. Some of the ashram inmates had not arrived.

Mother: "Where are the others?"

A brahmacharis: "Two people have some eye infection. They are resting."

Mother: " Are they lying down? They can't even walk?"

Br: "They have no trouble walking or anything. They are afraid that they may give you the infection, Amma."

Mother: "They don't need to worry about that! Whatever disease you children have, you can come near Amma. Son, people with all sorts of infectious diseases come to Her for darshan. How many people with eye infection, chicken pox, skin diseases have come to Her! She never had to break the routine of darshan so far. God always protected Her. She believes it will continue like that.

"Once, a woman devotee brought a glass full of milk. Amma drank the whole thing. A little later She began to vomit. She became very weak. Her body lost most of the water. But what She was thinking about was the crowd of devotees waiting for Her darshan. There were very poor people among them. They had to work as laborers for many days and save a few paise daily, to be able to have enough for the bus fare to come to see Her. If they had to go away without seeing Her, when will they get a chance again? Amma felt bad when She thought about them. She prayed and then sat up. She called the devotees near Her, consoled them and gave them the advice they needed. But by that time She began to vomit again. She closed the door, sat down on the floor and vomited. A little later, She changed Her clothes and started giving darshan again. After seeing ten people, She threw up again. When She was too feeble to get up, She imagined that She was singing a *kirtan* and dancing. That gave Her some energy. But then She would throw up again a little later. Again some darshan. This continued till the morning. She was very weak in the end. But She held on till She saw the last devotee. As soon as She gave darshan to the last person, Amma fell down. People carried Her to Her room. Every one was very worried, fearing that She might even die. If Amma was thinking only of Her own comfort, there was no need for any of this. She only had to go to Her room and lie down. She might have felt better very quickly. But when She thought of the sorrow of all the people who had come to see Her, She couldn't do that. She was ready to die if he had to.

"The milk given to Amma contained some poison. A family that was hostile to Mother had given the milk to a devotee to bring here. The devotee did not know that the milk was poisoned. She was not aware that the family which gave her the milk was opposed to Amma."

Amma gave the sweets to every one and then came downstairs. She sat down near the water tank on the south side of the meditation room. There were some sugar canes growing on the banks of the backwater near that spot. One of the canes was broken. A brahmachari cut it and brought it to Amma. She cut it into small pieces and gave them to the brahmacharis. As the sugar cane grew near salt water, its sweetness had a little salty taste. Mother also chewed a couple of pieces. Throwing out the residue, She said:

"Children, when you study the scriptures, you should remember this residue. We spit out the residue after we enjoy the juice of the sugarcane. In the same way, we should take the essence of the scriptures and discard the rest. It is foolish to cling to the scriptures till death. You should do the same with the words of mahatmas. We should accept only what we can assimilate and copy in our own lives. All their instructions are not equally suitable for everyone. They take into account the differences in the circumstances and the qualification of the listener when they give advice."

Mother walked towards the kalari. The devotees who were waiting rushed towards Her. She took them all into the kalari and sat down.

Mother's real form

A woman devotee prostrated to Amma and began to sob heavily lying in Her lap. Her grief was caused by the taunts she received from some people on the ferry. Amma wiped her tears and consoled her. Then She said to the devotees:

"If you pinch the trunk of a tree, it won't feel it. But if you pinch the tender new buds it will feel the pain. Amma would bear whatever anyone says about her. But if anyone gives pain to the devotees, if they say bad things about Her children,

Amma can't bear that. Even though all are really one atman, Amma can not stand aside when She sees the sorrow of Her children. Krishna did not flinch when Bhishma shot a hundred arrows at him. But when arrows sped towards Arjuna, when His devotee was going to be in danger, didn't Krishna jump towards Bhishma, wielding His chakra? Protecting the devotees is more important than one's own existence. That is what the Lord showed us."

A devotee: "Amma, is it not possible to eliminate those who malign God and berate the spiritual path?"

Mother: "Son, if we take such an attitude, we are more harmful than them. A spiritual person should never think of harming others. His prayer to God should be to give them good hearts and make them better. The aim of devotion and prayer is to get a mind that loves everyone. Anyway, don't feel bad about anyone maligning us, son! You have to think that it, too, is for the good. Is there a world without opposites? Isn't it because there is darkness that we know the greatness of light?"

Devotee: "How lucky we are to have come to you, Amma! There is only bliss when we are near you!"

Mother (Laughing): "Don't be so sure of that, children! You are all sick now. You all have wounds that are infected. Amma will squeeze them - to get the pus out. She will make your small mistakes look big. Then it will hurt a little. Amma tells Her children, 'Amma likes the Lord of Death more than Lord Shiva. Isn't out of the fear of death that people call out to Shiva? Otherwise who will take refuge in Shiva? At least out of fear of Amma, you will call God! (She laughs.) Earlier, the brahmachari children used to sing, '*Amme, snehamayi!*' (Amma who is all love!) Now they sing, '*Amme, kruramayi!*' (Amma who is all cruelty!)"

Mother laughs, and sings '*Amme kruramayi!.*', slowly, in tune. Everyone bends over with laughter.

Mother continues, "Sometimes, Amma will say that Her children are wrong, even when they are right. Why? Because they need to have shraddha. Then they will watch every footstep. They may be kicked or beaten up, but they won't react. They will stand there smiling. They often say, 'We like Amma to scold us a little. At least we can stand and watch Amma while She does that. It is even better if She spanks us a couple of times.' However much Amma chastises them, they know that She cannot help smiling at them the next moment. Now the only thing that works is for Amma to go on a hunger strike! They can't bear Amma going without food!"

No one spoke for a little while. They were all probably marveling at the care and affection that Amma gave to Her children which would be rare even in the mothers who gave birth to them. Slowly a woman devotee raised a question.

Surrendering to God

Devotee: "Amma, you say we have to see God in everything. But how is that possible?"

Mother: "Children, you have to get rid of all the vasanas that are in you. God has to become your only refuge. You have to develop the habit of remembering God, whatever you are doing. Then, slowly, you will begin to see unity in all this diversity."

A girl came forward and hugged Mother. Putting her head

on Mother's shoulder, she began to sob. She was the daughter of a truck driver. Her father was not usually at home. Her stepmother was pushing her towards an immoral life. She had finished high school, but no one wanted her to go to college.

Girl: "Amma, I have nobody! I will stay here and do some work."

Mother's eyes filled with compassion. She said, "Daughter, God is there always to look after us. He is the abode of compassion. He is our true father and mother. The persons we call our parents just brought us up. If they were our true parents, wouldn't they save us from death? But they are unable to do that. We existed even before we became their children. God is our real father and mother and protector."

Amma consoled the girl and gave her confidence. "Go home, daughter, and tell your father firmly that you want to go to college. He will agree. It is Amma who is telling you. Don't worry, daughter, don't worry!"

A woman devotee: "I want to come to see you daily, Amma. But I am alone at home. How can I come here, leaving the house unattended? Today, I locked the house and entrusted the key with my neighbor, before leaving."

Mother: "It is good to ask someone to watch your house when you come here. We do need to pay attention to external things. But aren't there thefts even when we use the most secure locks and employ guards to look after our homes? How can we explain that? They are not our guards in reality. Our true guard is God. If we put everything in His care, He will stay awake and protect it always. Other guards will fall asleep, and thieves will not miss the chance to steal our things. But when God is our guard, we have nothing to fear!

"Imagine that we got into a boat. We have a heavy bag. We are holding it up, in stead of putting it down. Seeing our struggle, the boatman says, 'You are in the boat now. Can't you put that bag down?' But we are not ready to do it. In stead, we are crying that the bag is too heavy. Is there any need for that? In the same way, why are we taking all these burdens on our heads? Put everything at the Lord's feet! He will take care of it all."

No time for sadhana

Meanwhile, Soman, a teacher, approached Mother with a question: "Amma, after school there are a hundred things to do at home. Where do I get time for japa?"

Mother: "Son, you will find time if you really want it. You need the conviction that remembrance of God is the greatest thing. Then you will find time even in the midst of all your work. Once a rich man went to his guru and complained, 'Master, my mind has no peace. It is always worried. What can I do?'

"The guru said, 'I will give you a mantra. You chant it regularly.' The rich man replied, 'But I have so many responsibilities throughout the day. How will I find time for chanting the mantra?'

"The guru asked, 'Where do you take your bath?' 'In the river.' 'How long does it take to get there?' 'Three minutes.' The guru said, 'Then you can chant the mantra from the time you start from home till you reach the river! Try that.'

"After a few months, the rich man came to see the guru in a very enthusiastic mood. He prostrated fully and said, 'My agitation is all gone. The mind is at peace. I regularly chant the mantra you gave me. Now it is impossible for me not to chant! First I started chanting on the way to the river. Then I practiced chanting on the way back and also while bathing. Then I started chanting on the way to work. Then, even while in my office, whenever the thought of the mantra came to mind, I began chanting. I chant as I go to bed. I fall asleep chanting. Now my desire is to chant more and more each day. I am unhappy when I am not chanting.'"

Mother continued: "You see, son, japa became a habit for him through constant practice. You should start getting up early. As soon as you get up, meditate for ten minutes. After your bath, you should meditate again for half an hour. In the beginning, it is enough to meditate for a short time. Then you may do your chores. Before going to the school, meditate again for half an hour. Whatever time is left after meditation should be used for japa. You can do japa while walking or sitting - while doing anything, for that matter. Amma is suggesting a discipline like this because you like spiritual life, son. Beginners need to meditate only for half an hour or an hour. The rest of the time can be used for japa and singing kirtans."

Soman: "Amma, how can I keep my mind on God? I have been married now for a year. I still have to repay the money I borrowed for building a house. My wife is not well. When all these problems bother the mind, how is it possible to do japa or meditation?"

Mother: "That is all true. But what is the use of your worrying, son? Will you get the money to pay off the loan? So be engaged in your karma, without wasting time. Try to chant your mantra all the time. Even if you forget at times, resume chanting as soon as you remember.

"If you water the tree at the roots, it will go to all the branches and the leaves. In stead, if you pour water on top of the tree, it will be of no use. There is nothing to be gained from worrying. But if you give your mind to God, if you take refuge in Him, you won't lack anything in life. You will get whatever you need. Problems will be solved, somehow. You will find peace. Those who pray to the Lord and meditate on Him sincerely will not feel shortage of anything that is essential. That is the Lord's resolve. That is Amma's experience. If nothing else, chant the Lalita Sahasranama daily with love and devotion. You won't lack anything. My dear children, whatever else you may have, you won't get peace of mind without doing sadhana. However rich you are, if you want to sleep peacefully, you have to take refuge in the Lord. Don't forget to think of Him, even if you forget to eat."

Complete surrender to God is the essence of Amma's teachings. Whatever our burdens are, if we surrender them to Him, their weight will not crush us. It is in the light of Her own experience that Amma says that the Lord will look after us in every way. Her answer to every question of a worldly nature raises us to the plane of devotion and spirituality. When Her blissful presence is combined with the sweetness of Her words of love, it becomes an unforgettable experience.

As Amma got up from Her seat, all the devotees prostrated to Her and got up also.

Saturday, November 2, 1985

Mother in Ernakulam

Mother and Her group stayed at the house of Her devotee, Gangadharan Vaidyar, near Ernakulam last night. This morning, they started for the home of another devotee in Eloor. On the way, they visited three more houses.

Many people had gathered in the house at Eloor to see Amma. A number of them were seeing Her for the first time. There were parents with retarded children, people who were maimed in some way, people who were searching for a job for years, spiritual seekers needing instruction in the method of sadhana, and those who wanted to lead a life of sannyasa at the ashram with Amma.

A devotee came forward with his son, who appeared to be about twelve. He prostrated to Amma and putting his son near Amma, he said,: "Amma, this boy is very naughty. He goes to the best school, but he displays his ability in making mischief only and not in his studies. He is just a puny kid, but he goes and asks a girl in his class to marry him! And he beats up the boy who reported this to the teacher. Amma, you should bless him and straighten him up."

Mother (hugging the boy): "What is this son, is your father telling the truth?" (She holds her finger at Her nose, as a gesture indicating 'Shame!') The boy was very ashamed and wanted to escape from Mother's grasp somehow. Amma didn't let him go. She made him sit in her lap and gave him an apple and planted a kiss on his cheek. She couldn't talk to his father for long as She only had a short time. She gave him permission to come and see Her later. He prostrated again, and departed.

Mother was already late for going to the Krishna temple near by where She was to lead bhajans. But she didn't get up before She gave darshan to everyone.

After the bhajan, She had to go to the houses of a few more devotees. It was very late by the time She got back to Vaidyar's house in Ernakulam. Although She had planned to return to the ashram at night, She yielded to the insistence of the devotees and decided to stay overnight.

The devotee who had brought his son to Her earlier in the day was waiting here to see Her again. He was losing hope of seeing Amma that night as it was very late. Then, a brahmachari indicated that Amma was calling him. He went to her and prostrated.

Devotee: "I had not expected to see Amma tonight at all."

Mother: "Amma had planned to leave tonight itself, but decided to stay overnight, since all the children here insisted. Some children are waiting for Her in Haripad. We will see them tomorrow, on the way back. When Amma came here, She felt you were unhappy. Son, you don't have to worry about your boy. All his mischief will disappear as he grows older."

Devotee: "Amma, but the children today do things that I couldn't even think of when I was young. I can't understand the reason for this, however much I think about it."

Let dharma begin at a young age

Mother: "Son, in the old days children grew up in gurukulas under the direct supervision of the guru. They lived with the guru. They were taught how to respect the guru, how to behave towards the parents and how to live in this world. They were taught what the essence of God was. Not only were they taught these things, but they were also made to follow them. The foundations of education was service to the guru, tapas, and study of the scriptures. Because of this, that age could create persons like Harishchandra. What was King Harishchandra like? He showed that his word was greater than his wealth, his wife and his child. That is the ideal that the people of old have set before us. It was the result of the education they got. When children returned from the gurukula after their education and entered *grihasthashrama*, their parents entrusted them with all the responsibilities and entered the stage of *vanaprastha* (forest recluse). Even a king would just wear a single piece of cloth and go to the forest to do tapas. He would not retain any of the trappings of royalty. They lived with the goal of sannyasa in mind. Most of the people then had the desire to give up everything somehow and enter a life of sannyasa. Because of this culture, the children of those days became rooted in their dharma and full of courage as they grew up. They could go forward without faltering in any circumstance."

Devotee: "Amma, but it is just the opposite now. In the children, day by day our culture is decaying."

Mother: "How can good qualities grow in the children nowadays? How many householders observe the tenets of their stage of life properly? How can they instill good qualities in their children? In the old days, the householders indeed led the life of true grihasthashramis. They found time to do tapas even in the midst of all their work. They did not think that life was just for eating and drinking. They ate just to maintain life. They would impart good advice to their children, and they would set a model by living in accordance with their advice. But who does such things nowadays? Where are gurukulas now? Even in nursery schools, the children are shouting slogans. There is politics even in those schools. There are strikes. One sees even in children the readiness to kill members of opposing parties. Thus they are being brought up in a destructive manner.

"The son who ought to nurse and console his father who is old and sick, demands his share of the property, in stead. When the homestead is divided, his brother's share happens to have a few more coconut trees, so he draws a knife to stab his father. The son is ready to kill his father for a little bit of wealth! But what did Sri Rama and others showed us? To keep his father's word, Rama was ready to give up the kingdom. And, Dasaratha, his father did not deviate from his word, either. He kept the promise he had given his wife, Kaikeyi. And that promise was given in return for a great sacrifice. What impressed Dasaratha at that time was not his wife's beauty or show of love, but her selflessness in the battlefield where she risked her own life to save him. He did not sacrifice his word for selfish reasons later. And Rama unconditionally accepted his father's word.

"And what about Sita? Did she make a big fuss when Rama decided to go to the forest? She didn't say to him, 'You shouldn't go to the forest. You are the heir to the kingdom. You should get it by whatever means.' Her husband went to the forest and she followed him silently. And his brother Lakshmana accompanied them. And what did Bharata show us? He didn't say, 'They are all gone. Now I can rule the kingdom.' He went in search of his brother. He got Rama's sandals, brought them back and put them on the throne. He then ruled the country on Rama's behalf. That is how it was during the old days. That is the model that we should emulate in our lives. But who is paying attention to those things now or putting them into practice?

"The ancients taught us the true principles. But we don't pay attention to them. And we see the deficiencies arising from that neglect. What kind of culture do the children get today? You find only TV and cinema everywhere. They deal with romance and sex and marriage mostly. Magazines and books deals mostly with worldly matters. Children see and read these things. That is the culture our young ones get. This will help make only people like Kamsa. We will hardly see Harischandras in the future.

"If we want any change to this, we have to pay special attention to our children. We have to be very careful about what we give them to read. We should give them only things that will help them in their studies or explain spiritual matters. And we should even put pressure on them to read such things. That culture will stay with them even when they grow up. Even when they do something wrong, they will have an awareness of that deep within and they will come to regret their action. This will change their minds.

"Many children see TV and the movies and dream about a married life like that depicted there. How many people can lead the happy, luxurious life of the stories? And when they can't get that, there is disappointment and the partners grow distant. Once a young woman came to see Amma. She had married when very young and was divorced already. When Amma asked the reason, she told the story. She had seen a movie about a rich couple. Big house, a car, expensive clothes. They drove to the beach in the evenings. Never a moment that was not full of happiness. After seeing the movie, the girl began dreaming about all this. Soon she was married. But the husband had only a small job. There wasn't enough money and he could not afford the kind of life his wife desired. She wanted a car, more and more saris, daily trips to the movies and so on. She was always disappointed. What could the poor husband do? Finally, they began to fight. It came to blows. They were both unhappy. So the marriage was dissolved. That brought more despair than ever. They were regretting all that happened. What could they do?

"Think of the old days. Then, the couples were ready to die for each other. They loved each other. Though separate in bodies, they were one at heart. Children, selflessness and love are the wings of married life. They help us soar high into the sky of happiness and contentment."

Mother looks very carefully at even those things that others may not consider very significant. She ignores Her own comfort and convenience and gives Her utmost attention to suggesting solutions to the problems of Her children.

The devotee, who had listened to Amma's words carefully, said: "I want to put into practice at home all the things you said. Give me your blessings, Amma!"

Mother: "Son, no action that is undertaken with shraddha will be a waste. No word will be a waste. If not today, tomorrow you will get the benefit from it."

Mother sows the seed and goes forward. Some of them sprout tomorrow and some the day after. Some may sprout only years later. Even if no one is there to hear it, Mother

Nature keeps a record of each of our sincere prayers. "Make the effort, children, Mother is with you!"

Sunday, November 3, 1985

Retarded children - whose karma causes their disability?

Mother and the brahmacharis started from Gangadharan Vaidyar's house at six-thirty in the morning. On the way, the brahmacharis started talking about the retarded children who had come to see Mother the day before.

"The plight of those children is very pitiable. Their bodies are growing up, but their minds are not growing at all. What a life!"

"Their parents' case is even more pitiable. Do they have any freedom in life? Can they leave the children and go any where with peace of mind?"

"Whose prarabdha is this, the child's or the parents'?"

In the end they decided to ask Amma. She was listening carefully to the conversation of Her children.

Mother: "Those children live as if in a dream, more or less. They are not aware of the suffering that we see in them. Only if they are aware of it, they will feel sorry for themselves thinking, 'Alas, why I am in this world in this condition?' They don't have that awareness. It is their families that suffer. They are the ones who face the difficulties. So we have to think it is mainly the prarabdha of the parents."

Br: "Poor parents! What can they look forward to, in this life? What can we do for them?"

Advice to the brahmacharis

Mother: "Children, this very compassion that you feel for them will bring peace to them. It will enlarge your hearts also. We need to have compassion for the suffering of others. The deeper a well is, the more water it can hold. Only compassion will cause the well spring of the paramatman to issue forth, children! That supreme principle awakens due to compassion.

"Even when they sit down for meditation, some people are thinking of how to take revenge for something. Children, you cannot build a house just by piling up bricks; you need cement to hold them together. Love is that cement. You cannot tin a vessel which is not clean. It has to be rubbed clean first. Likewise, only when the mind is clean, devotion will take root in it and we can enjoy the presence of the Lord. Think of Kuchela. His children were starving and he went to beg for food. As he was coming back, someone else held out his hand, crying that his family was starving. Kuchela gave him whatever food he had received.

"Don't you know the story of the sage Durvasas and King Ambarisha? The sage went to break Ambarisha's vow and if he couldn't do that, he wanted to curse the king. But Ambarisha was a sincere devotee. Even though Durvasas became very angry with him, Ambarisha remained in the attitude of a servant of the sage, without reacting in any way. He was aware of his own powers, but he did not voice any opposition to the sage. With joined palms, he prayed to Durvasas, 'Please forgive me if I have committed some error! I was only trying to maintain my vow. Forgive me for my ignorance!' But Durvasas did not forgive him. He decided to kill him, instead. But before that, Lord Vishnu's *sudarshana chakra* came to Ambarisha's rescue.

"Terrified by the sudarshana, Durvasas ran to the gods for help. When he left, Ambarisha, on his part, did not think, 'Oh, he is gone. Now I can eat something in peace!' Durvasas couldn't get any help from any of the devas. He had no escape but to seek refuge in Ambarisha himself. Even when the sage came and begged his forgiveness, the king wanted to wash his feet and drink that water! God is with only such people. He will come to help those who have that kind of humility. Those who think, 'I want to be happy; I want to be rich; I want liberation!' are not going to find God on their side."

Mother stopped talking, and silently looking out through the small window on the right side of the vehicle. A lorry went by, blaring its horns. They were speeding past trees and houses. Time was lurching forward. All eyes were on Amma. A brahmachari broke the silence, and called. "Amma!"

"Yes, what do you want?," Mother responded in a detached tone.

The brahmachari lowered his tone and said, "I feel sorry that I made Amma angry the other day!"

Mother: "But that is all past. Why do you worry about it now? Amma forgot it right away. Wasn't it out of love for you that Amma spoke so sternly then, son?"

Tears started flowing from his eyes. Amma wiped them with Her sari, and said: "Don't worry, my darling!"

The other day, Amma had asked him to clean the verandah of the kalari before leaving the ashram. But in his hurry to travel with Her, he had forgotten to do that. Mother noticed the verandah as She was ready to leave. It was still dirty. She called the brahmachari and scolded him severely. She started to clean the place Herself. Seeing this some others came to help Her. The brahmachari stood there with his head lowered in guilt. Mother left the ashram only after cleaning the whole area.

Mother continued: "When Amma says something sternly to you children, it is not because She is angry inside. It is to keep you from becoming egoistic. Amma would like to do all the chores Herself. She would like to do that as long as She is healthy. But She tends to forget sometimes. Only because of that, She asks you to pay attention to certain things. Amma would like to wash her own clothes. Even now She tries to do that, but Gayatri doesn't let Her. Amma doesn't like to give trouble to any one.

"Amma likes to do service, not to receive it. She doesn't need any service. But, sometimes, She has to accept service for the happiness of others. Even then, Amma is thinking only of what is good for you children.

"You are all luckier than most other people. You don't need to worry about anything. Amma is there to take care of all problems. She is there to hear about your sorrows and to console you. There is a saying that one should get out in the world only after attaining realization. But this doesn't apply to those who have reached a satguru. A disciple sent out by a satguru does not have to fear anything. The guru is there to protect him!"

A brahmachari who was listening to all this asked: "Amma, you have said often that a person can experience the Self in three years' time. What kind of sadhana do you prescribe for that?

To be fit for realization

Mother: "One who has intense yearning doesn't need three years. Why, he doesn't need even the time it takes to pierce a lotus leaf with a needle. But, his longing, his suffering for realization should have the utmost intensity. With each breath, he should be crying out to God, 'Where are you?' He should reach a state where he can't live any longer without attaining God.

"Some people don't gain anything even after doing tapas for fifty or sixty years. If you follow what Amma says, you can certainly attain your goal in three years. But you need shraddha. You need true *lakshya bodha*, and true dedication. Amma is talking about people who have that. If you catch an ordinary bus, you can't be sure when it will reach the destination. It will stop at a lot of places. But if you catch an express bus, you can tell when it will reach there. It won't stop here and there. We can't be sure of those whose detachment lasts only for two days.

"Son, when the thought that you are born dies, that is self-realization. When you are convinced that you are the true Existence without birth, growth and death, that is realization. That is not something that you can get from somewhere else. You have to get your mind under control - that is what is needed.

"Do you know what Amma's life was like? She wouldn't even leave Her footprints when sweeping the front yard. And if footprints were somehow made, She would sweep them off. God's footprints must form there first! There was the conviction that God was walking there. If She happened to take even one breath without remembering God, She would cover Her nostrils to stop breathing, think of God and only then resume breathing. And while walking, She would take each step only after remembering Him. If, at any step, She couldn't do it, She would take a step back, remember God and only then go forward.

"Don't you know the story the man who went in search of 'tampran's' lion? We have to get that kind of intensity[17]. Constantly we should be searching, 'Where are you? Where are you?' Because of the intensity of this search, everywhere it would get so hot that God will not be able to sit peacefully! He has to come before us. Before starting meditation, Amma used to decide for how many hours She would sit. She wouldn't get up before that. If She couldn't sit for that long, She would charge at Mother Nature, roaring, ready to beat Her up! At night, She wouldn't sleep at all. If She felt sleepy, She would sit there and cry. She didn't feel sleepy usually. When the time came to sleep, She would grieve that one more day was being wasted. Amma can't even stand the memory of that. It was so hard."

---

[17] 'Tampran' is respectful term used by the members of lower caste while referring to the those of higher castes. The story that Amma is referring to is this: An illiterate forest dweller made friends with a yogi. The yogi spent most of his time in deep meditation on the Lord Narasimha, the man-lion incarnation of Lord Vishnu. Seeing his great longing to get a vision of the Lord, the forest dweller took pity on him and went in search of the man-lion. His search became very intense. He gave up food and sleep and rest and tirelessly sought the man-lion for his friend with an innocence, intensity and yearning that finally forced Lord Vishnu to appear before him as Narasimha. The man tied a noose around the Lord's neck and brought him to the yogi, with no inkling of the fact that it was none other than the Supreme Lord he had captured. The Lord gave instant moksha (liberation) to the forest dweller while the astonished yogi got a promise of liberation in this birth itself.

Br: "If a normal person doesn't sleep, wouldn't that disturb his meditation, Amma?"

Mother: "One who is pining for the knowledge of God will not stop thinking about Him even for an instant. He wouldn't feel sleepy. He wouldn't lie down. Even if he did, his grief will keep him awake. Amma was talking about such people. For those who have detachment and the desire to know God, tapas is the real form of rest. There is no rest beyond tapas. Those who do that don't really need sleep. We are aiming for that state."

Brahmachari: "Doesn't the Gita say that one who sleeps too much and one who doesn't sleep at all will not attain yoga?"

Mother: "Amma is not saying that you should give up sleep completely. You should get enough sleep - but just enough. A sadhak will not be able to sleep when he remembers his goal. He will not lie down to sleep. He will go on with his japa and fall asleep unknowingly. The children who want to pass the examination will not feel like sleeping. They will stay up at night and study. That happens naturally. Such an attitude comes naturally to a sadhak.

"The children who really love Mother should imbibe the principles She teaches. They should readily sacrifice anything to live according to those principles. Those are the ones who really love Mother. The aim of such a person is to adhere to those principles unfailingly, even if that means facing death. In stead, one who just mouths the words, 'Amma, I love you' does not really love Her.

"A king has two servants. One of them hangs around the king, without attending to any of his duties. The other man spends every hour of the day doing the things the king asks him to do. He toils without food or sleep. He doesn't worry whether the king sees it or knows about it. Who is the better of these two? Whom would the king like more?"

Mother's true nature

Mother continued to speak, explaining Her own nature further.

"The river flows on by itself. It purifies everything that joins it. It doesn't need the water from the pond. You don't have to love Amma for Her sake. Amma loves you all. Thinking of your own good, She may not show that love, sometimes. Amma doesn't show any love to Gayatri, outwardly. But when she is not near, Amma's eyes fill with tears at the very thought of Gayatri as She thinks of her hard work and suffering. What Amma loves is that daughter's mind and her actions. And that love comes by itself. Amma is not consciously bringing it on. But She doesn't display that love even for a second. She finds fault with everything that Gayatri touches or does. She doesn't even address her as 'mol' most of the times. Often Amma thinks, 'Am I really so cruel that I cannot sow my compassion outwardly! I am always making her suffer!' Even if Amma decides at night to show Her love to Gayatri the next day, She actually ends up scolding her for something or other. She has woken Gayatri up from sleep and made her stand up. She has put her outside and closed the door. She has punished her in many ways like this. But all this is not because Amma doesn't love her enough. Amma's love for Her is full. She is after her mind. But Gayatri has never wavered a bit. That is real prema."

Brahmachari Pai raised a doubt at this point: "Amma, you

often say that a sadhak should not have close connections with worldly people; he shouldn't use their clothes and other things or go into their bedrooms. Then how can he do service?"

Rules for doing service

Mother: "There is no harm in doing service. But one shouldn't lose shraddha. It is all true that everything is the same Self, all is God and God is in everyone and in everything. But one should act with discrimination according to the circumstances. When a sadhak visits a house, he should not go to the bedrooms as far as possible. If you go to a place where coal is handled, even if you don't touch it, some of the coal will stick to you. It is said that if you go to Kurukshetra you can still catch the sounds of the ancient battle which took place there. In the rooms used by worldly people, the vibrations of their thoughts will be present. If you use those rooms, those vibrations will enter at least your subconscious mind. And you will suffer the bad effects of that, sooner or later. So if you visit a home, as far as possible, stay in the puja room and talk to the family members there.

"In your conversation, avoid worldly matters. It is best not to talk about anything that is not spiritually beneficial. Conversation about unnecessary subjects is like a whirlpool; it will pull our minds down without our knowledge. The clothes that others wear will contain the vibrations of their thoughts. Therefore, sadhaks should not wear the clothes used by worldly people. It is not good to use their soap, either. If you give your soap to someone, it is better not to take it back. Take the necessary clothes and your seat wherever you go.

"Sadhaks should not maintain unbreakable ties to any one, especially to householders. But our conduct should not be such as to hurt them. If they insist on something, explain your point in a few words, with a smile. After a certain stage in sadhana, these things will not affect a seeker much. Seekers will remain unaffected just as a lotus leaf when water falls on it. Even then, one should stay alert."

Mother reached Haripad by noon, after visiting the homes of some devotees and a branch of Her ashram in Ernakulam. Prof. N.M.C Warrier and family had waited for Her all night without sleep. Amma had said She would arrive last night. Since they had decided not to eat before She came, no one in the family had eaten anything. Amma gave them the chance for a good meditation. What would the Lord not do to keep the devotee's mind firmly tied to Him?

To welcome Mother, the host's son had drawn some *'kalams'* - a traditional designs on the floor, drawn with rice flour and turmeric powder - and lit an oil lamp at the center of it. Amma looked at the design carefully and said: "There is a small error in this. One shouldn't make any mistake while making a *kalam*. It is said that if you make a mistake, there will be strife in the family. We draw these things with a certain samkalpa. Son, you should first practice it in sand. Measure every thing and make sure it is correct. Only after you have practiced well, you should draw a kalam. What you have done is all right now because it was done with a pure heart full of love and devotion for Amma. But you should pay attention next time."

Amma visited five more houses in Haripad. Whenever She went to a house, the neighbors would invite Her to visit them also. However tired She is and whatever pressure others put on Her to take some rest, Amma would go to all those houses. In the bliss they derive when the dust from Her holy feet sanctify their homes, the devotees forget Amma's troubles.

Many devotees were waiting for Amma at the ashram since the morning. Although She was very tired physically, Amma did not break the schedule of bhava darshan.

Monday, November 4, 1985

It was three in the afternoon. Amma was in Br. Sree Kumar's room, sitting near him on his bed. He had fever for the last two days. A brahmachari brought hot water in a container for Sree Kumar to steam himself. The mouth of the container was covered by tying a banana leaf tightly across it.

Mother: "Get down on the floor, son. Steam yourself a little. You will feel better."

She helped him sit up on the bed. A grass mat was put on the floor. Amma held Sree Kumar's hand and made him sit on the mat. He was covered with a thick sheet.

Mother: "Son, you break the cover of the pot now. Steam yourself till you sweat really well. Then the fever will go."

Some devotees who had come for Mother's darshan came to the hut, hearing that She was there.

Mother: "Sree *mon* has fever for two days now. Amma thought of giving him a steam treatment. When did you children come?"

A woman: "A while ago. Only just now we came to know that Amma is sitting here."

Mother removed the sheet that was covering Sree Kumar. He had sweated well. She helped him to get back on the bed and lie down. Amma was talking to the devotees. After some preliminaries, the conversation turned to more serious matters.

Vedanta - the true and the false

A devotee: "Amma, the other day a friend of mine visited me. He is in love with the wife of a friend of his. While talking about it, he says, 'Kabirdas gave his wife when someone asked him, didn't he? So what is so wrong in this?'"

Mother: "But didn't Kabirdas give his wife away happily to the one who asked? He didn't betray his friend and steal his wife. Let this person who talks Vedanta ask his friend if he is ready to give away his wife. He may not be around much longer. (Laughs). Kabir was a righteous person. For him, his dharma was greater than his wife or himself. So he wouldn't have hesitated at all. His habit was to give whatever any one asked. He didn't budge from his dharma even when someone asked for his wife. But a wife has her own dharma. A wife who is really devoted to her husband will not even look at another man's face. Ravana stole Sita. He tried to tempt her in so many ways. But she didn't waver; she thought only of Rama. She decided that she would not yield to another man even if that meant she had to die. That is a wife's dharma.

"What we see in Kabir is the sign of a liberated being. He had given up all notions of 'I' and 'mine'. Everything is the Self or God. This is the attitude a spiritual person should have. He should see everything as God; or else, he should see everything as himself. In one view, everything is the Lord. Then there is no hatred or anger towards any one. There is only worship. In the second view, nothing is distinct from one's own self; there is no second person. Remove the boundary between two fields; then there is only one field. One sees oneself in everything. Just as the right hand comes to dress the wound on the left hand, one sees the another man's sorrow as one's own sorrow and goes to his aid."

A brahmachari was going to Ernakulam for a couple of days to buy some things. He picked up an umbrella from the hut. It had no handle and the cloth had faded a little. He put it back. There was a new umbrella hanging behind the door. The brahmachari took that one, in stead. He prostrated to Mother and went out of the hut, ready to start his trip.

Amma called him back. She took the new umbrella from him and asked him to take the old one he had looked at. The brahmachari did so without any hesitation and went out. Every one watching was perplexed by this. When asked about it, Amma said: "He didn't want the old umbrella, only the new one! A brahmacharin's mind should not be trapped by external glamour. It is to get rid of the attachment to luxuries that one lives in the ashram."

But a few moments later, Amma asked someone to call the brahmachari back. She took back the old umbrella and gave him the new one again. He prostrated to Her again and got up.

Mother: "Son, a spiritual seeker shouldn't go after external beauty. That is perishable. It will ruin him also. He should look at the inner beauty. That is what is eternal. That will make him grow. Only if he discards the external totally, he can make progress. Amma is giving you the new umbrella back because She sees in you an attitude of surrender that lets you accept the good and the bad equally. You chose the better umbrella to get the approval of others, didn't you? Don't be attracted by the praise of others. If you wait for the certificate of approval from others, you won't receive the certificate from God! What we need really is God's certificate. For that you have to withdraw the mind that is looking outward and turn it inward. You have to search and discover that which is within.

"I will pay attention to every side of my children's lives. I will look at even little things. Who is there but Amma to rectify even your small mistakes? But your attention should not be in external glitter. Your mind should be focused on God."

Amma is there to pay close attention to even the seemingly unimportant things in Her children's lives. Then why should they attend to external things? This is Amma's attitude.

Mother's bhakti bhava

Mother: "Amma's voice is gone after these last two or three days of travel. There was no rest. Now it is difficult to sing bhajans even. Amma hasn't had this much trouble any time in all these years. What is the use of the tongue, if one can't sing bhajans?"
Br: "You took over the prarabdha of those who came to see you at Eloor, Amma! That is what caused this. How many sick people had come there! And they were not the same when they went back. They went away smiling."
Mother: "If my pain is the result of their prarabdha, if I am now suffering what they were meant to suffer, then I am not unhappy. After all someone else is being cured. But even then, I cannot spend a day without uttering the Lord's name!"
Amma's eyes were full. Tears started flowing in a steady stream. She was the true picture of a devotee who was lamenting with

an aching heart her inability to repeat God's name. And the surroundings, bathed in the red hue of the dusk, seemed to mirror Her mood of sorrow. The sublime mood of Her glowing *prema bhakti* - devotion that is pure love - seemed to enhance the radiance of Amma's face. Her sorrowful sobs gradually subsided. Amma slipped into a state of samadhi. This state lasted for about an hour.

Every one there had a lesson from Mother on how to call out and cry for God. A little while after waking up from the samadhi, Amma came to the kalari and joined the bhajan.

Kannante Kalocha ...

> *I heard Kannan's footsteps*
> *On a silvery moonlit night.*
> *I heard the notes of his flute,*
> *And my mind merged*
> *In a golden dream!*
>
> *Oh, Fragrance of Winter,*
> *Flowering in the whiteness*
> *of the silvery moon!*
> *My mind shines blissfully*
> *In that honey-sweet smile!*
>
> *O Kanna,*
> *I have countless tales to tell*
> *Kanna, please don't go!*
> *Please stay for a bath*
> *In the blissful lake of my mind!*

When Mother returned to her room, a brahmachari was waiting for Her. His eyes were swollen. His whole face had changed.

Mother: "What happened to you, son!"

Br: "It started this morning. My face is swelling up."

Mother: "There is nothing to fear. There is swelling because some dust has fallen in your eyes."

Amma asked a brahmacharini to bring some rose water. When she brought it, Amma asked the brahmachari to lie down on the floor. She gave him Her pillow to put his head on. But he was reluctant to place his head on it.

Mother: "True reverence for Amma is not refraining from using these things because they belong to Her. Amma doesn't see it that way. The sign of reverence for Amma is in your obedience to Her."

She put the reluctant brahmacharin's head on the pillow and poured some rose water in his eyes. She asked him to lie still for a while.

Friday, November 8, 1985

Brahma muhurta

The morning star rose. As the brahmacharis got up, lights from their huts filtered out through the gaps in the thatched-leaf walls. Amma passed in front of each hut, with a flashlight in hand, to check that Her children were up. Most of the brahmacharis had taken their bath. Vedic mantras echoed in the air.

There was no light in one of the huts. Mother shone the flashlight inside. The brahmachari was sound asleep. Amma tugged at the corner or of the sheet which was covering him. He turned to the other side and pulled back the sheet and covered himself again. Amma was enjoying this. She pulled the sheet again. He pushed away Her hand that was holding the sheet and curled up again. Mother got some water in a cup from outside and approached Her son again. She sprinkled water on his face.

He jumped up and looked around with the irritation of the broken morning slumber. Two piercing eyes in front! Even in his half-asleep state, it didn't take him any time to recognize that form clad in pure white. He stood up trembling. When she saw that he was up, Amma's smile faded. She now wore the mask of seriousness.

Mother: "During archana, all the deities come here. Are you lying here to get their curse? If you can't even get up in the morning, why come to live in the ashram? Why not go and hitch up with some girl and live happily? When the kids cry day and night for some thing, you can sing to them and put them to sleep on your shoulder. Only then people like you will learn!"

Mother was not ready to stop Her tirade. "How many days has it been since you went for archana?"

The brahmachari said, faltering: "Two days." He couldn't raise his head and look at Amma.

Mother: "You should be ashamed to say that. Even Achamma, who is past seventy, gets up at 4:30!"

The brahmacharis who returned from archana saw Amma in Her aspect as Kali. They prostrated in front of Her. But, as Amma came out of the hut, Her mood changed totally. She put on a pleasant, smiling, auspicious face. She sat down with

Her children near the darshan hut. Where is that ferocious mood that was seen just seconds ago? Within an instant, Her lotus face had blossomed with a smile of tender love.

Mother: "I asked him why he was staying here if he could not obey the ashram rules and do his sadhana. It must have hurt him. It pains Amma to scold you children. But it is Amma's rebukes more than Her love that removes the dirt in you. If Amma shows only love, you won't look inside. Amma's rebuke is nothing but Her full love for you. It is Her compassion. It is real love, children. You maybe upset when Amma chastises you. But Amma is doing it to weaken your vasanas and to awaken your real self. There is no way to remove the vasanas without a little pain. The sculptor chips away the rock with his chisel to bring out the real form that is inside - and not because he is angry at the rock. The iron smith heats up the metal and beats on it only to give it the desired shape. Similarly, for an infected abscess to heal, you have to squeeze it and get the pus out. Sometimes, the doctor may cut it open. Those who look on may think the doctor is so cruel. But, if out of his affection for the patient, the doctor just puts some medicine without hurting him by cleaning the abscess, it will not heal at all. In the same way, the guru's rebukes and disciplining may give some pain to the disciple. But his aim is only the removal of the disciple's vasanas.

"Children, when the cow eats the young coconut sapling, no use telling her gently, 'Don't eat it, my dear!' But if you shout at her, 'Shoo! Go away', she will stop eating the tree and move away. Amma's word have to make the intended transformation in you. That is why Amma takes on such a serious mood."

In the case of the ashram inmates, who but Amma was

there to love them and scold them and even to wield the cane and give them a taste of it if necessary?

Amma remained silent for a few moments and then continued: "Children, if you are upset, Amma will stop scolding you. Amma likes to see you happy. She doesn't want to hurt you!"

Hearing these words, the brahmacharins' hearts fluttered. Each time Amma took them to task, their love for Her deepened further and their bonds only became stronger.

Mother got up and walked to the dining room. She continued talking to the brahmacharis who followed Her like Her shadow.

Mother: "Amma is not talking in this serious tone with the intention of hurting you. It is to let you see for yourselves how strong your bond with Amma is. Only those who will stay on in spite of even being beaten and killed will progress! A brahmachari is one who has to carry the whole world on his shoulders. He should not be weakened by little things. I will really shake my children up. Those who desire only self-realization will stay, others will leave."

Yes, fortunate are those who remain at Her feet even when the compassionate Devi takes Her fierce form.

Mother recounts old stories

In the kalari, the evening bhajan was going on.

Ottoor had been hoping for a couple of days to spend some time near Amma. He slowly walked to Amma's room now. He became very happy when he saw Her. She took hold of his hand to make him sit near Her. Ottoor prostrated to

Her and putting his head in Her lap, he lay down like a little baby. Amma stroked his back with affection. Ottoor's nephew Narayanan and another brahmachari were in the room.

Ottoor raised his head from Amma's lap and said: "The brahmacharis come and tell me the stories about the old days. My regret is that I was not fortunate enough to see those things with my own eyes. It would be enough if I could listen to you recount those stories, Amma! They told me that your family tied you up and beat you. When I heard that, little Ambadi Kanna[18] came to mind. Why were they beating you?"

Mother laughed and started recounting: "Those days, Amma used to bring some food to the poor people around us, even if She had to steal from home. That is what they beat Her for. Amma would go to the houses of those neighbors to collect tapioca skins and *kadi*[19] to feed the cows. In most of those houses people would be starving. Amma would feel sorry for them. She would take a pot and put some boiled rice in it when no one was watching. She would pretend that she was going for *kadi*, and take the rice to the neighbors who were starving. In some families, the grandmothers weren't given soap and other things. Amma would bring them soap from Her own home. She would wash their clothes for them."

Ottoor: "Oh, they were people who had earned much merit. They could take part in Amma's leelas!"

Mother: "Amma did all these things, but later She felt an intense detachment from everything. She didn't like anyone coming near Her and hindering Her meditation. She felt an

---

[18] The little Krishna of Ambadi. 'Ambadi' (*literally* cowherds' village in Malayalam) is the village where Krishna grew up.
[19] The water in which rice has been washed

aversion towards everything. She couldn't stand even Mother Nature. She hated Her own body. She would bite and wound it. She would pull out Her own hair. She would remember only later that she had done those things to herself."

Ottoor (with surprise): "Did your parents see all these things?"

Mother: "When Amma's father saw her crying loudly, he would come and lift Her up on his shoulder. He had no idea why Amma was doing these things or crying. One day, Amma told him, 'Take me to some secluded place. Take me to the Himalayas!', and She started crying. Amma was very young then. Her father put Her on his shoulder to stop the crying, and said, 'I will take you there just now. Get some sleep now, my child!'

Suddenly Mother slipped into a deep samadhi. Her hands were still, locked in some mystical *mudra*. Only the sweet rhythm and harmony of the bhajan from the kalari broke the silence.

Amba Mata Jaganmata.

> *O Divine mother, Mother of the Universe,*
> *O Most courageous Mother*
> *Giver of Truth and Divine Love!*
> *O Thou who art The Universe Itself,*
> *Thou who art Courage,*
> *Truth and Divine Love!*

The bhajan reached its highest pitch. One could tell that the brahmacharis were totally immersed in the singing, forgetting all else. Amma remained in the state of samadhi. Slowly the song came to an end. The instruments slowly became silent.

The harmonium was now being tuned for the next kirtan. Amma slowly came out of the sublime mood and assumed Her normal state. The conversation continued.

Ottoor: "How old were you then?"

Mother: "Seven or eight. Amma's father put Her on his shoulder and walked around. Hadn't he said that he would take Her to the Himalayas? She believed it totally, just as any child would do. And She fell asleep on his shoulder. When She awoke, She started crying again, seeing that he had not taken Her to the Himalayas. Those days my father went through a lot of trouble. I would meditate sitting in the courtyard at night, without sleep. Father would also stay up watching me. He was afraid to leave his daughter alone there at night.

"Amma used to go to get things to feed the goat. There was a large tree leaning over the water. She would climb the tree and sit there. Suddenly She would feel that She was Krishna. She would sit there swinging Her legs. Quite naturally, She would begin to make the sound of a flute. As She broke branches of the tree and dropped them, other girls would gather them. Amma would imagine that they were the gopis. These thoughts came to Her mind naturally. She would wonder whether She had gone crazy. Amma usually went alone to fetch water. Her family didn't want Her to go with others. One day She suddenly climbed the banyan tree and lay there on a branch, like Lord Vishnu lying on Ananta[20]. On a very slender branch. It didn't break. That tree is still there on the sea shore."

Ottoor: "You would climb up and lie on a thin branch?"

Mother: "Yes. Just like the Lord on Ananta. Those who

---

[20] Ananta is the great serpent who serves as the bed on which Lord Vishnu rests.

watched used to say things like there were different colors on Amma's body. She doesn't know. That was probably there faith. Amma cannot even think of that world now."

Ottoor: "I would like to hear the story where Amma turned water into panchamritam[21]."

Mother: "Amma made those who had no faith themselves do it. She didn't do it Herself. There were many people then who didn't have faith in Amma. It was the period when bhava darshan had started. Amma asked some of the people who opposed Her, to bring some water. They brought water in a jug. She asked them to imagine that it is transforming. The water turned into panchamritam right there, in their own hands.

The bhajan ended in the kalari. The mantra invoking peace resounded everywhere.

> *Om purnamadah purnamidam*
> *purnat purnamudachyate*
> *purnasya purnam adaaya*
> *purnam evavashishyate*
> *Om shanti shanti shantih*
> *Om Shri Gurubhyo Namah! Harih Om*
>
> *That is the Whole, this is the Whole;*
> *From the whole, the whole arises;*
> *Taking away the Whole from the Whole,*
> *The Whole remains…*
> *Peace, Peace, Peace!*
> *Salutations to the preceptors! Harih Om!*

---

[21] A sweet pudding made of milk, bananas, raw sugar, raisins and rock sugar.

There was silence everywhere for a few moments. Then the bell for arati started. Narayanan helped Ottoor get up and walk to the kalari to see the arati. The brahmachari walked backed to his room with a feeling of enrichment having witnessed that scene where love-filled devotion on one side and deep motherly affection for the devotee on the other combined so beautifully.

Glossary

Achyuta: "The Imperishable One; The Everlasting One." One of Vishnu's names.

Adharma: Unrighteousness, sin, opposed to Divine Harmony.

Advaita: Non-dualism. The philosophy which teaches that the Supreme Reality is "One and indivisible."

Ahimsa: Non-injury, non-violence. Refraining from hurting any living creature by thought word or deed.

Ambika: "Mother." The Divine Mother.

Ammachi: Mother.

Anna prasana: The first feeding a baby is given of solid food.

Annapurna: The Goddess of Plenty. A form of Durga.

Arati: The ritual in which light is offered in the form of burning camphor, and a bell is rung before the Deity in a temple or a holy person, as a consummation of puja (worship). The camphor does not leave behind any residue, which symbolizes the total annihilation of the ego.

Archana: "Offering for worship." A form of worship in which the names of a deity are chanted, usually 108, 300 or 1000 times in one sitting.

Asana: A small mat which the aspirant sits on during meditation. Yoga posture.

Ashram: "Place of striving." A place where spiritual seekers and aspirants live or visit in order to lead a spiritual life and practice sadhana. It is usually the home of a spiritual master, saint or ascetic, who guides the aspirants.

Atman: The true Self. The essential nature of our real existence. One of the fundamental tenets of the Sanatana Dharma is that we are not the physical body, feelings, mind, intellect or personality. We are the eternal, pure, unblemishable Self.

GLOSSARY

AUM: Sacred syllable. The Primordial Sound or Vibration, which represents Brahman and the entire creation. AUM is the primary mantra and is usually found at the beginning of other mantras.

AVADHUT: A Self-realized soul who, seeing only the unity of everything, has transcended all social conventions.

AVATAR: "Descent." An incarnation of the Divine. The aim of a God-incarnation is to protect the good, destroy evil, restore righteousness in the world, and to lead mankind towards the spiritual Goal. It is very rare for an incarnation to be a full descent (Purnavatar).

AYITHAM: The Malayalam word *ayitham* (from the Sanskrit *asuddham*) refers to the observance of the belief that a person of high caste is defiled by the approach or touch of a person of certain low castes.

AYURVEDA: "The science of life." Ancient Indian, holistic, health and medicinal system. Ayurvedic medicines are usually prepared from medicinal herbs and plants.

BHAGAVAD GITA: "God's Song." Bhagavad = of the Lord; Gita = song, referring particularly to advice. The teachings which Krishna gave Arjuna on the Kurukshetra battlefield at the beginning of the Mahabharata war. It is a practical guide for man's daily life and contains the essence of Vedic wisdom.

BHAGAVAN: The Blessed Lord; God. According to Vedanga, a branch of Vedic literature, Bhagavan is He who destroys transmigratory existence and bestows union with the Supreme Spirit.

BHAGAVATA: See Srimad Bhagavatam.

BHAJAN: Devotional singing.

BHAKTI: Devotion.

BHAKTI YOGA: "Union through bhakti." The Path of Devotion.

The way of attaining Self-realization through devotion and complete surrender to God.

BHASMA: Sacred ash.

BHAVA: Divine mood.

BHAVA DARSHAN: The occasion when Mother receives devotees in the exalted state of the Divine Mother. In the early days, Mother also appeared in Krishna bhava.

BHIKSHA: Alms.

BIJAKSHARA: A seed letter in a mantra.

BRAHMACHARI(NI): A celibate disciple, who practices spiritual disciplines and is usually being trained by a Guru.

BRAHMACHARYA: "Abidance in Brahman." Celibacy and discipline of the mind and the senses.

BRAHMAN: The Absolute Reality; the Whole; the Supreme Being, which encompasses and pervades everything, and is One and indivisible.

BRAHMA SUTRAS: Aphorisms by Sage Badarayana (Veda Vyasa) that expound Vedantic philosophy.

CHAMMANDI: Coconut chutney.

CHANDALA: Outcast.

CHECHI: (Malayalam) "Older sister." It is more affectionate to call someone "Chechi" than by their name.

DAKSHAYANI: A name of the Divine Mother Parvati.

DARSHAN: An audience with or a vision of the Divine or a holy person.

DEVI: "The Effulgent One." The Goddess

DEVI BHAVA: "The Divine Mood of Devi." The state in which Mother reveals Her oneness and identity with the Divine Mother.

DHARA: A continuous stream of liquid. The term is often used to denote a form of medical treatment by which a medicinal liquid is poured continuously over the patient. It is also a form of ceremonial bathing of the icon of a deity.

DHARMA: "That which upholds the universe." Dharma has many meanings, including, the Divine Law, the law of existence, in accordance with divine harmony, righteousness, religion, duty, responsibility, right conduct, justice, goodness and truth. Dharma signifies the inner principles of religion.

DHYANA: Meditation, contemplation.

DIKSHA: Initiation.

DOSHA: Pancake made of rice flour.

DURGA: A name of Shakti, the Divine Mother. She is often depicted as wielding a number of weapons and riding a lion. She is the destroyer of evil and the protector of that which is good. She destroy the desires and negative tendencies (vasanas) of her children and unveils the Supreme Self.

DWARAKA: The island city where Krishna lived and discharged his kingly responsibilities. After Krishna left his body, Dwaraka was submerged in the ocean. Archeologists have recently discovered the remains of a city in the ocean near Gujarat, which is believed to be Dwaraka.

EKAGRATA: One-pointed concentration.

GAYATRI: The most important mantra in the Vedas, associated with the Goddess Savita. Upon being given upanayana, one is supposed to chant this mantra. Also, the Goddess Gayatri.

GITA: Song. See *Bhagavad Gita*

GOPALA: "Cowherd Boy." One of Krishna's names.

GOPI: The gopis were cowherd girls and milk maids who lived in Vrindavan. They were Krishna's closest devotees and were known for their supreme devotion to the Lord. They exemplify the most intense love for God.

Grihasthashrami: A grihasthasrami is someone who is dedicated to a spiritual life, while leading the life of a householder.

Guna: Primal Nature (Prakriti) consists of three gunas, i. e., fundamental qualities, tendencies or stresses, which underlie all manifestation: sattva (goodness, purity, serenity), rajas (activity, passion) and tamas (darkness, inertia, ignorance). These three gunas continually act and react with each other. The phenomenal world is composed of different combinations of the three gunas.

Guru: "One who removes the darkness of ignorance." Spiritual master/guide.

Gurukula: An ashram with a living guru, where disciples live and study with the guru.

Guruvayoor: Place of pilgrimage in Kerala, near Trissur, where there is a famous Krishna temple.

Haimavati: A name of the Divine Mother Parvati.

Hatha Yoga: A system of physical and mental exercises, developed in ancient times, with the purpose of making the body and its vital functions into perfect instruments, in order to help one attain Self-realization.

Homa: Sacrificial fire.

Hridayasunya: Heartless.

Hridayesha: the Lord of one's heart.

Japa: Repetition of a mantra, a prayer or one of God's Names.

Jarasandha: The powerful king of Magadha, who fought 18 battles with Lord Krishna, and was killed by Bhima.

Jivatman: The individual soul.

Jnana: Spiritual or divine wisdom. True Knowledge is a direct experience, beyond any possible perception of the limited mind, intellect, and senses. It is attained through spiritual practices and the grace of God or the Guru.

KALI: "The Dark One." An aspect of the Divine Mother. From the viewpoint of the ego, She may seem frightening because She destroys the ego. But She destroys the ego and transforms us only out of Her immeasurable compassion. Kali has many forms; in Her benevolent form, She is known as Bhadra Kali. A devotee knows that behind Her fierce facade, the loving Mother is to be found, who protects Her children and bestows the grace of Liberation.

KAMANDALU: A kettle with a handle and bent nozzle, used by monks for collecting water and food.

KAMSA: Lord Krishna's demonic uncle whom he killed.

KANJI: Rice gruel.

KANNA: "He who has beautiful eyes." A nickname of Krishna as a baby. There are many stories about Krishna's childhood and he is sometimes worshipped in the form of a Divine Child.

KAPHA: See "Vata, pitta, kapha."

KARMA: Action, deed.

KARMA YOGA: "Union through action." The spiritual path of detached, selfless service and of dedicating the fruit of all one's actions to God.

KARMA YOGI: A karma yogi follows the path of selfless action.

KARTYAYANI: A name of the Divine Mother Parvati.

KAURAVAS: The one hundred children of Dhritharasthra and Gandhari. The Kauravas were the enemies of the Pandavas, who they fought in the Mahabharata War.

KINDI: A traditional bronze or brass container with a spout, usually used for worship.

KIRTAN: hymn.

KRISHNA: "He who draws us to himself," "the Dark One." The principal incarnation of Vishnu. He was born into a royal family, but grew up with foster parents and lived as a young cowherd in Vrindavan, where he was loved and worshipped by his devoted companions, the gopis and gopas. Krishna later became the ruler of Dwaraka. He was a friend of and adviser to his cousins, the Pandavas, especially Arjuna, to whom he revealed his teachings in the *Bhagavad Gita*.

KRISHNA BHAVA: The state in which Mother reveals Her oneness and identity with Krishna.

KUMKUM: Saffron.

KSHATRIYA: The warrior caste.

KSHETRA: Temple; field; body.

KUNDALINI: "The Serpent Power." The spiritual energy, which rests like a coiled snake at the base of the spine. Through spiritual practices it is made to rise through the sushumna canal, a subtle nerve within the spine, and move up through the chakras (power centers). As the kundalini rises from chakra to chakra, the spiritual aspirant begins to experience finer levels of consciousness. The kundalini finally reaches the highest chakra at the top of the head (the Sahasrara Lotus), which leads to Liberation.

LAKSHYA BODHA: Constant awareness of, and intent on, the Supreme Goal.

LALITA SAHASRANAMA: The thousand names of the Divine Mother in the form of Lalitambika.

LEELA: "Play." The movements and activities of the Divine, which by nature are free and not necessarily subject to the laws of nature.

MAHATMA: "Great soul." When Mother uses the word "mahatma," She is referring to a Self-realized soul.

Mahasamadhi: When a realized soul passes away, it is known as mahasamadhi, "the great samadhi."

Mala: Rosary, usually made of rudraksha seeds, tulasi wood or sandalwood beads.

Mantra: Sacred formula or prayer which is constantly repeated. This awakens one's dormant spiritual powers and helps one to reach the goal. It is most effective if received from a spiritual master during initiation.

Mantra diksha: Mantra initiation.

Mataji: "Mother." The suffix "ji" denotes respect.

Maya: "Illusion." The Divine Power or veil with which God, in his Divine Play of Creation, conceals himself and gives the impression of the many, thereby creating the illusion of separation. As Maya veils Reality, she deludes us, making us believe that Perfection is to be found outside of ourselves.

Mookambika: The Divine Mother, as she is worshipped in a famous Devi temple in Kalloor, South India.

Mukti: Liberation.

Muladhara: The lowest of the six chakras, situated at the base of the spine.

Mudra: Sacred hand sign or gesture, which represents spiritual truths.

Nanda: Krishna's foster father.

Narayana: Nara = knowledge, water. "He who is established in Supreme Knowledge." "He who dwells in the causal waters." Name of Vishnu.

Nasyam: A cleansing ayurvedic treatment, which consists of a nasal infusion of medicated oil.

Ojas: Sexual energy transmuted into subtle vital energy through spiritual practices.

Om Namah Shivaya: The Panchakshara Mantra (mantra

consisting of five letters), which means, "Salutations to Shiva, the Auspicious One."

PADA PUJA: The worship of God's, the Guru's or a saint's feet. As the feet support the body, the Guru Principle supports the Supreme Truth. The Guru's feet thus represent the Supreme Truth.

PANDAVAS: The five sons of King Pandu and heroes of the epic Mahabharata.

PARAMATMAN: The Supreme Spirit; Brahman.

PARVATI: "Daughter of the mountain." Shiva's divine consort. A name of the Divine Mother.

PAYASAM: A sweet rice pudding.

PEETHAM: Sacred seat.

PITTA: See "Vata, pitta, kapha."

PRADAKSHINA: A form of worship in which one circumambulates in a clockwise direction a holy place, a temple or a holy person.

PRARABDHA: "Responsibilities, burdens." The fruit of past actions from this and past lives, which will manifest in this life.

PRASAD: The consecrated offerings distributed after puja. And whatever a mahatma gives, as a sign of his blessing, is considered prasad.

PREMA: Supreme love.

PREMA BHAKTI: Supreme love and devotion.

PUJA: Ritualistic worship.

PURNAM: Full, perfect.

RADHA: One of Krishna's gopis. She was closer to Krishna than any other gopi and personifies the highest and purest love for God. In Goloka, the celestial abode of Krishna, Radha is Krishna's Divine Consort.

Rajas: Activity, passion. One of the three gunas or fundamental qualities of Nature.

Rama: "The Giver of Joy." The Divine hero in the epic, *Ramayana*. He was an incarnation of Vishnu, and is considered to be the ideal of virtue.

Ramayana: "The life of Rama." One of India's greatest epic poems, depicting the life of Rama, written by Valmiki. Rama was an incarnation of Vishnu. A major part of the epic describes how Sita, Rama's wife, was abducted and taken to Sri Lanka by Ravana, the demon king, and how she was rescued by Rama and his devotees.

Rasam: A broth made with tamarind, salt, chilies, onion and spices.

Ravana: The demon king of Sri Lanka, who is the villain in the Ramayana.

Rudraksha: The seeds of the rudraksha tree, which have both medicinal and spiritual power, and are associated with Lord Shiva.

Sadhak: A spiritual aspirant who practices sadhana for the purpose of attaining Self-realization.

Sadhana: Spiritual disciplines and practices, such as meditation, prayer, japa, the reading of holy scriptures and fasting.

Sahasrara: "Thousand-spoked" (lotus). The highest chakra, situated at the top of the head, wherein the Kundalini (Shakti) unites with Shiva. It resembles a lotus flower with a thousand petals.

Samadhi: Sam = with; adhi = the Lord. Oneness with God. A state of deep, one-pointed concentration, in which all thoughts subside, the mind enters into a state of complete stillness in which only Pure Consciousness remains, as one abides in the Atman (Self).

Sambar: A broth made of vegetables and spices.

Samsara: The world of plurality; the cycle of birth, death and rebirth.

Samskaras: Samskara has two meanings: Culture and the totality of impressions imprinted in the mind by experiences (from this or earlier lives), which influence the life of a human being—his nature, actions, state of mind, etc.

Sanatana Dharma: "The Eternal Religion." The traditional name for Hinduism.

Sandhya: Sunrise, midday, or sunset—usually sunset.

Sankalpa: A creative, integral resolve which is manifested. The sankalpa of an ordinary person does not always yield the corresponding fruit, but a sankalpa made by a Self-realized being inevitably manifests its aimed result.

Sannyasi: "A monk or nun who has taken formal vows of renunciation. A sannyasi traditionally wears an ochre colored cloth representing the burning away of all attachments.

Satguru: Self-realized, spiritual master.

Satsang: Sat = truth, being; sanga = association with. Being in the company of the wise and virtuous. Also a spiritual discourse by a sage or scholar.

Shakti: Power. Shakti is also a name of the Universal Mother, the dynamic aspect of Brahman.

Shastri: Religious scholar.

Shiva: "The Auspicious One; the Gracious One; the Good One." A form of the Supreme Being. The masculine Principle; the static aspect of Brahman. Also the aspect of the Trinity associated with the destruction of the universe, the destruction of that which is not Real.

Shraddha: In Sanskrit, Shraddha means faith rooted in wisdom and experience, whereas the same term in Malayalam means dedication to one's work and attentive awareness in every action. Mother often uses the term in the latter sense.

SRI or SHREE: "Luminous, holy." An honorable prefix.

SHRIDARA: "He who holds Lakshmi." A name of Vishnu.

SRIMAD BHAGAVATA: One of the 18 scriptures known as the Puranas, dealing with the incarnations of Vishnu, especially, and in great detail, the life of Krishna. It emphasizes the path of devotion.

TAMAS: Darkness, inertia, apathy, ignorance. Tamas is one of the three gunas or fundamental qualities of Nature.

TANDAVA: Shiva's dance of bliss, especially at dusk.

TAPAS: "Heat." Self-discipline, austerities, penance and self-sacrifice; spiritual practices which burn up the impurities of the mind.

TAPASVI: One engaged in tapas or spiritual austerities.

TENGA: Coconut in Malayalam.

TIRTHAM: Holy water.

TYAGA: Renunciation.

UPANAYANA: The traditional ceremony in which a child born to upper caste parents is given the sacred thread and initiated into sacred studies.

UPANISHADS: "To sit at the feet of the Master." "That which destroys ignorance." The fourth and concluding part of the Vedas, which deals with the philosophy of Vedanta.

VADA: a savory, deep-fried, patty made of lentils.

VAIRAGYA: Detachment.

VANAPRASTHA: The recluse stage of life. In the ancient Indian tradition, there are four stages of life. First the child is sent to a gurukula where he (or she) lives the life of a brahmachari. Then he gets married and lives as a householder, dedicated to spiritual life (grihasthashrami). When the couple's children are old enough to take care of themselves, the parents retreat to a hermitage or an ashram, where they live a purely spiritual life, doing spiritual practices. During the fourth stage of their lives, they renounce the world completely and live the life of sannyasis.

VARNA: Major caste. The four major castes are Brahmin, Kshatriya, Vaishya, and Sudra.

VASANA: From "vas" = living, remaining. Vasanas are the latent tendencies or subtle desires within the mind which have a tendency to manifest into action and habits. Vasanas result from the impressions of experiences (samskaras) which exist in the subconscious.

VATA, PITTA, KAPHA: According to the ancient science of ayurveda, there are three primary life forces or biological humors, called vata, pitta and kapha, corresponding to the elements of air, fire, and water. These three elements determine the life processes of growth and decay, and are the causative forces in the disease process. The predominance of one or more of these elements in the individual determines his psycho-physical nature.

VEDA: "Knowledge, Wisdom." The ancient, sacred scriptures of Hinduism. A collection of holy texts in Sanskrit, which are divided into four parts: Rig, Yajur, Sama and Atharva. They are among the world's oldest scriptures. The *Vedas* are considered to be the direct revelation of the Supreme Truth which God bestowed upon the Rishis.

VEDANTA: "Veda-end." The philosophy of the *Upanishads*, the concluding part of the Vedas, which holds the Ultimate Truth to be "One without a Second."

VEENA: An Indian string instrument which is associated with the Divine Mother.

VRINDAVAN: The place where the historical Krishna lived as a young shepherd.

VYASA: The Sage who divided the one *Veda* into four parts. He also composed 18 *Puranas* (epics), the *Mahabharata* and the *Brahma Sutras*.

YAGA: Elaborate Vedic sacrificial rite.

YAJNA: Offering.

YAMA AND NIYAMA: The do's and the don'ts on the path of yoga.

YASHODA: Krishna's foster mother.

YOGA: "To unite." A series of methods through which one can attain oneness with the Divine. A Path which leads to Self-realization.

YOGI: Someone who is established in the practice of Yoga, or is established in union with the Supreme Spirit.

5